Tri–Coastal

and Other Poems

Written by
M. A. Katz–Savoy

Photography by
Kristina L. A. Schlah

M. A. Katz–Savoy
Kristina L. A. Schlah

Tri–Coastal and Other Poems

MLMC–Gothic and Main
Northampton, MA

Published by MLMC–Gothic and Main
29 Butler Place, #2
Northampton, MA 01060
http://www.mlmc-media.com

Cover photograph by Kristina L. A. Schlah
Cover design and other images by MLMC Media.
Gothic and Main logo by Renetta Hood.
"Tri-Coastal II" and "Richard the Poet at 3 AM" by Melissa Goldsmith

ISBN 978-1-63328-004-5

Dedication

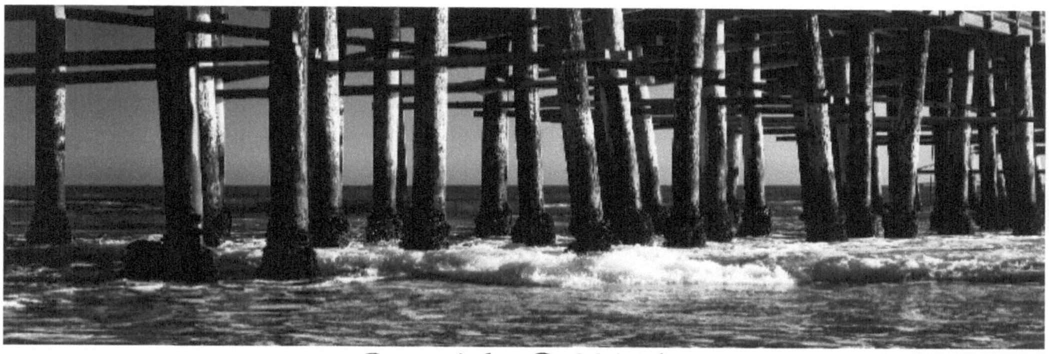

Copyright © 2014 by Kristina L. A. Schlah

I wish to dedicate this book to all my favorite English teachers who encouraged me to write poetry. I am sorry it took so long to hear your voices. I also express my gratitude to Kristina L. A. Schlah, whose beautiful photographs are featured in this book, and to the Gothic and Main folks at MLMC Media. Writing for Gothic and Main has been an absolute pleasure.
—M . A. Katz–Savoy

This book is dedicated to my mom, who encouraged my art every step of the way and gifted me with my best cameras, and to my dad, from whom I inherited my affinity for black and white photography. Also to my brother Erich, my sister Nicole and Keenan, Melissa and Tony, Gothic and Main (MLMC Media), M. A. Katz–Savoy for the immense honor of entrusting me to bring photographic images to her extraordinary poetic words, Swim Club (the first rule about Swim Club is that you do not talk about Swim Club), the entire Squashed Grapes cast and crew, the Nunley family, the Ross family, Judy, Tanya, Cindy, Laura (love, light, peace . . .).

And to Daniel: "True love stories never have endings."
—Richard Bach
—Kristina L. A. Schlah

CONTENTS

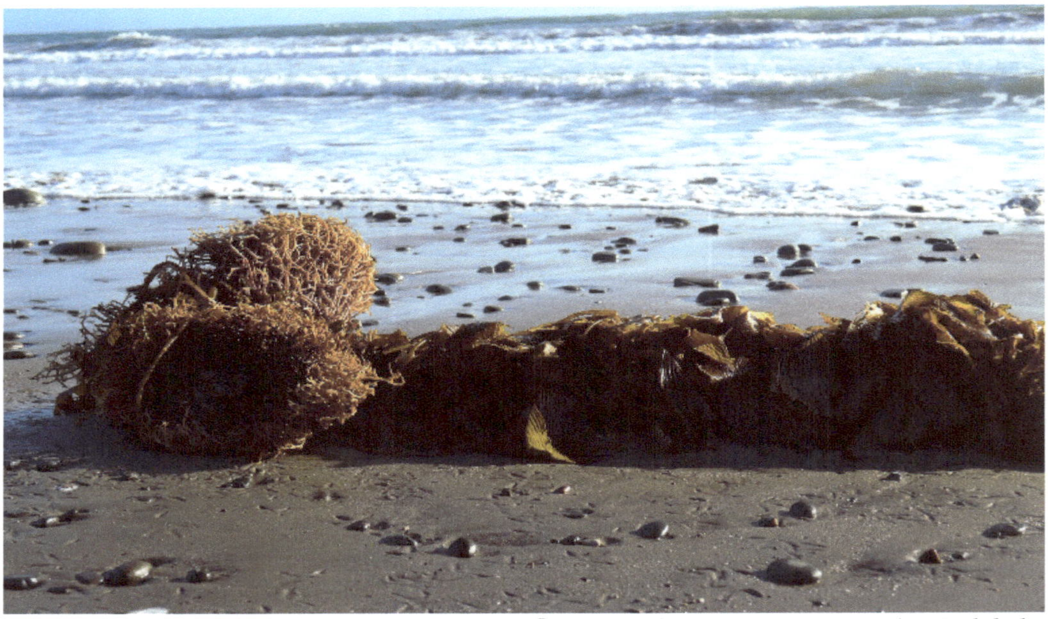

Tri–Coastal

I.

On whirlwind,
tracing a triangle,
West–East–South,
South–West–East,
East–South–West,
a topographical dance—a three–point turn,
waltzing on gigantic bodies of water.

I Pivot:
For opportunity—
For greener grass—
For difference—
For memories—
For three lives to merge into one:
Two visitors; One native.

Raised by the Pacific's turquoise waves,
taught by the Atlantic's pitch–black ocean,
toiled by the Gulf's brownish–gray water,
came up for air in the West, and
placed loved ones below earth in the South.
Found life in the East—again.

An odd triptych—
Vertical, Horizontal, Vertical,
Latitude, Longitude, Latitude . . .
with water in every picture,
and wave, after wave,
drawing this moon child like a crab,
to touch each shore.

I have drawn many crescents,
with airplanes, cars, passenger trains:
To live—
To visit—
To learn—
To answer,
"Where are you from?"
"Are you from here?"
"Where y'at?"

I have laughed
at the poor, shut–in soul,
stored in one place.
She ignores her restlessness,
closes her mind,
touches one body of water,
never dares to reinvent.

I have thought
of my many friends
who've lived on one coast.
They travel to other places,
but never live anywhere new.
Their lives
seem in stasis.

"If you live on two coasts,
you must be in show business—
Drawn to motion pictures,
drawn to theatre. . . .
But what do you do
To find yourself on three coasts?
Do you play new roles everyday?"

It's that third coast
that's my third eye:
Through it I learned to see
sounds of the blues,
music to dig a deep hole,
to people more ancient
than their ages can tell.

Did you know
that on each coast
even sound sounds different?
It isn't just the drawls,
the conservation of "r,"
the dropped final consonants,
the talking through the nose.

Each coast has its Foley editor,
West—he favors his figure–eight mic,
East—he lets the soap star clink her jewelry,
South—he adds some pink noise
to accompany the yellow filter
that is screwed tightly on the camera's lens.

Have I lost depth?
Does wading on three coasts make me shallow?
Tri–coastal, I drift in like water.
It may have turned me
fickle as a moonstone,
but I find myself
fitting in
both well–traveled native
and "from somewhere else."

Maybe nobody likes a changeling,
but I've managed to have good friends
on three coasts.
They help me lose myself
in their worlds.
I get to be Carl Rogers
anywhere I want.

A scholar of life,
it's best not to be connected
to place or space.
I carry my heart.
I can blow with the wind—a weed seed.
The monarchs may pass me by,
but never will I land inland.

II.
Bop!
The sinewy melody
I play has a
wide, open canvas
with three distant parameters
and my horn can take you there
all in one night.

You'd think we'd start with
the East Coast,
but that is not from where
my music originates.
It comes from the West,
rising up
out of the Camarillo Mental Hospital.

It drives itself up
the Pacific Coast Highway
and loiters with nude bodies
at Gaviota.

Adding to this imagery,
my horn presents to you
pointillistic granules of sand.

In—
This—
Hard—
Groove—
We go—
Up the PCH
to swing with the *Dharma Bums*.

My horn
calls the time.
My horn
is the train.
My horn
is the trip.

From the Cascades
to Seattle,
this night train
becomes quiet,
but scenic,
since it is your first hint
of the seasons.

Pike Place Market,
a view of Elliott Bay.
My horn is a vapor
of freshly made coffee
that warms you
in that glorious moment
in the middle of my fog.

Don't get settled.
For the flight is now happening.
This is the real modulation.
This is beyond tonal implication.
Here we find reminiscence,
and a Dixieland tease.
Let us go dancing in New Orleans.

Louis and King Oliver
are there,
but my horn won't let you forget
Lil Hardin—
Here's a segment of "Just for a Thrill,"
and another from "Oriental Swing."

We've taken ourselves
to the French Market
to admire the artisan's work,
laugh at a young boy's flap ball changes,
correct his sorry riffs,
and fall into his breaks.

As we go to Memphis,
we get innovative by the river
in an imaginary recording studio.
Here is my echo.
Here is my reverb.
Elvis has left the building.

You've seen Chicago
a million times before.
You've got a hint of it
in New Orleans, so . . .
we take ourselves deeper South instead,
walking through Delius' orange groves.

This passage—
Composed here—
Touches the feistiest ocean.
Can't you hear
the cold waves?
I'd give you a colorful animal,
but my horn does not offer goofy images.

This is the Atlantic.
Our pace changes as we
exit the Virginia corridor.
We speed past Howard,
and cross the Duke Ellington Bridge,
on the other side,
we meet him, but keep up our pace.

Hot jazz!
I have taken his "Ko–Ko"
as my own and I've hinted at
his "Blue Ramble."
But I must improvise
and my horn must be free.

And just when you believe this song
has become organized,
with a hint of Latin jazz,
my horn flies you
to another destination:
New York.

The heroin's a dream—
The heroin's a scream—
The heroin courses through my veins,
up through my warm breath,
into the horn
and past open keys—
Escapes euphoria,
finding your ears.

Stay with me and my silver spoon.
We'll busker with the Beats,
who don't get my horn,
but like musicians and free spirits
who bring their own demons
to the ceremony.

From nightclub to nightclub,
my horn gives you a snapshot
of heritage, smoke, and
Harlem Renaissance.
The Atlantic turns
this fantasy black and tan.

Another rest in Boston,
then to Vermont and Maine.
To Portland we go
to walk in the sand,
which isn't like the West Coast or the Gulf at all,
is it?

Coda from a horn player:
Morning is here
and it's time to take care
of some unfinished business
about trips to three coasts,

funny drinks,
and your tips.

Pay me well and return tonight.
My horn will be ready
to do the tour another way.
I'll dash my t's and dot my i's
to that promise.
I'll take you there.

III.

Nobody wants to die in the South.
Some may call it home,
but the South is no resting place
for visitors in transition.

From November to February,
the magnolia and red bud trees
begin to bloom.
And gentle myrtles drop
last petals of pink, purple, magenta, and white.

The heat will be gone
and Cottonwood trees will drop their pods,
just so you can make them crunch
with your rubber boots.

Nobody wants to die in the South,
when his or her heart is by
the Pacific or the Atlantic,
and we can't eat Gulf seafood anymore.

Stay inside for Christmas
because those layaways
will get you run over
by a shopping cart.

Mardi Gras makes little sense
if it's all parades
and not getting your fingers stomped
picking up beads for just an hour.

No snow may be good for the lungs,
and the humidity good for the skin.
The rent is cheaper than anywhere else,
but none of these things mean stay.

Nobody wants to die in the South.
But the pacemaker is in,
a promise of any better life.
At least being homeless by an ocean
brings you closer to cleaner sea air.

Nobody wants to die in the South.
But I couldn't fly you out anywhere else.
It all happened slowly,
but also too fast.
Your marble headstone is beautiful.
wish you were here.

IV.
The tide goes out,
and the people I know
all go away.

When it comes in again,
no matter which coast,
they welcome me back.

They have no idea
that they're the ones
who leave.

I select a color of the water,
wait for the moon to act. . . .
The waves do the rest.

They come in to play,
to complicate life,
to ignore me.

My mind gives them roles:
The best ones
are hoofers, teachers, painters, strummers.

Some are characters
I want to throw back,
to drown and get lost at sea.

In this parallel universe,
I am always at home,
a Viewmaster with three different wheels.

On three coasts,
I get to be beautiful,
and I greet you every time.

You know me,
I love mischief and I like to play,
though I'm mutable and you can't catch me.

You think me your muse,
the way you think I come and go,
but you are really mine.

Let's run around pylons,
take snapshots of algae,
let's recreate our escapades

On three coasts . . .
and again,
and again,
and again.

How funny to be greeted:
"Where are you from?"
"Are you from here?"
"Where y'at?"
I am here all the time.

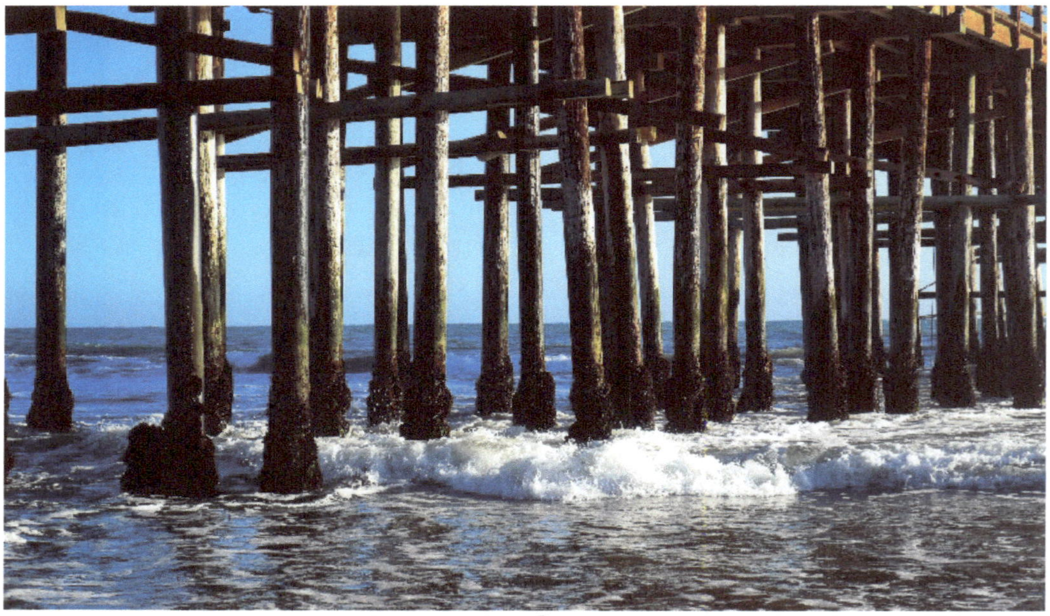

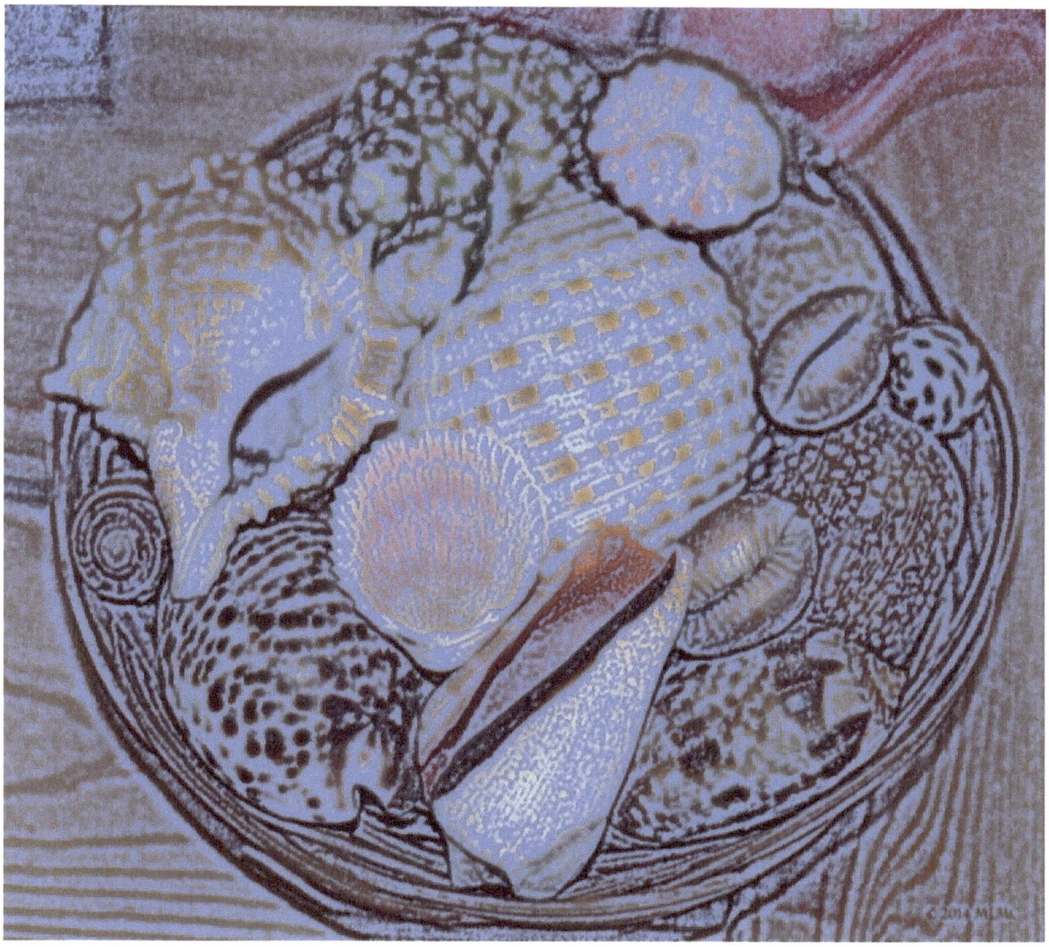

Tri–Coastal 1:
Texas and Louisiana

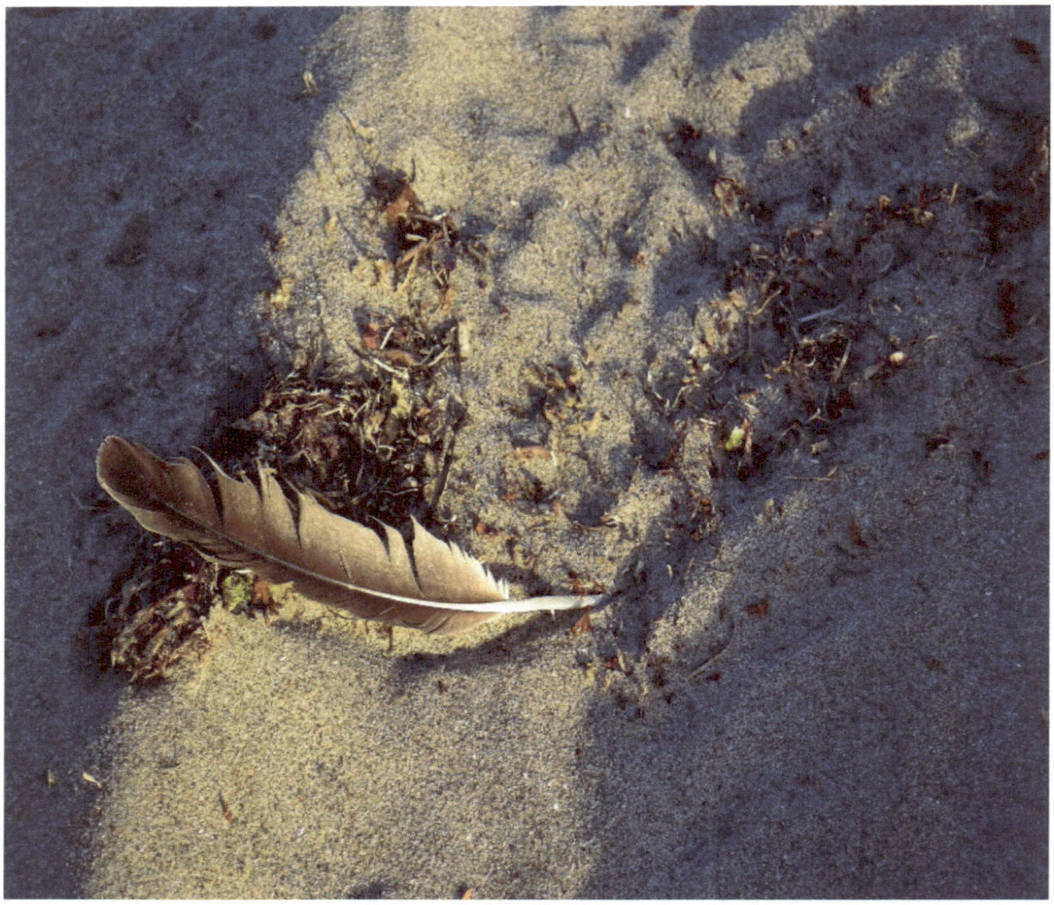

Certain Slant

The sun's five fingers reach
through silver–lined clouds.
Transformed, the dark greens
of Texas hills and trees.
Brushstrokes that restore
the earth's distressed canvas.

They must have seen it.
Ancestors must have named it.
Miracle, God in the searchlights.
They must have thought
the outstretched hand
a personal greeting,
a friendly shoulder tap,
a gentle massage
after a long day.

I drive over one hill
towards another, indiscernible.
My windshield covered now—
Dust of the past,
remnants of memories,
long–gone friends.

The rays stretch out.

Into the Dragon

When I was a child
I used to think
the lights on the towers
windows
so round and so white
or stacks
of gold coins, a gilded city.

At day break, the stench
makes unmistakable
despite the fog
that slashes the tops
of buildings and towers
the oil refinery.

The Sunshine Bridge
stretches
across the Mississippi
It is a steel
dragon
straddling both banks
steam seeps from the
land itself
thick smoke that blinds.

We aim our headlights
at the lair's entrance,
accelerate
to ascension
our headlight beams
into the maw
of the metal beast.

Speeding towards the apex
the arched steel spine

Downward
We roll to the tail.
Where it guards
Towers of steam,
stacks
of gold.

And there
we slay or are slain.

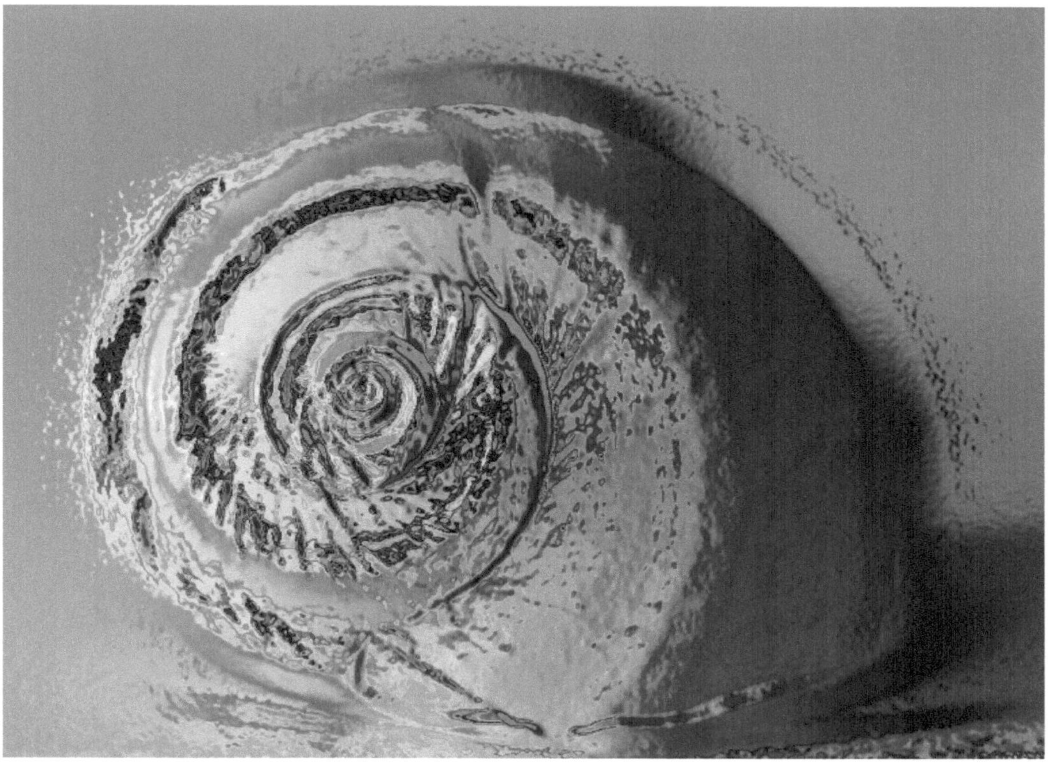

The Other Side

the railroad divides worlds
St. Anthony's lost children:

a homeless beggar
scraggly beard
local radio–ad T–shirt

the words
                    "Fear This"

across his chest

crosses the tracks
joins others

                    huddled beside a brick shelter

under the overpass,

                              they sleep

without blankets,
without pillows,
without sheets

                              in fetal positions,
hands between legs
                    or
on their backs,
hands crossed serenely

ants crawl around and over them

nearby pigeons
fight for scraps

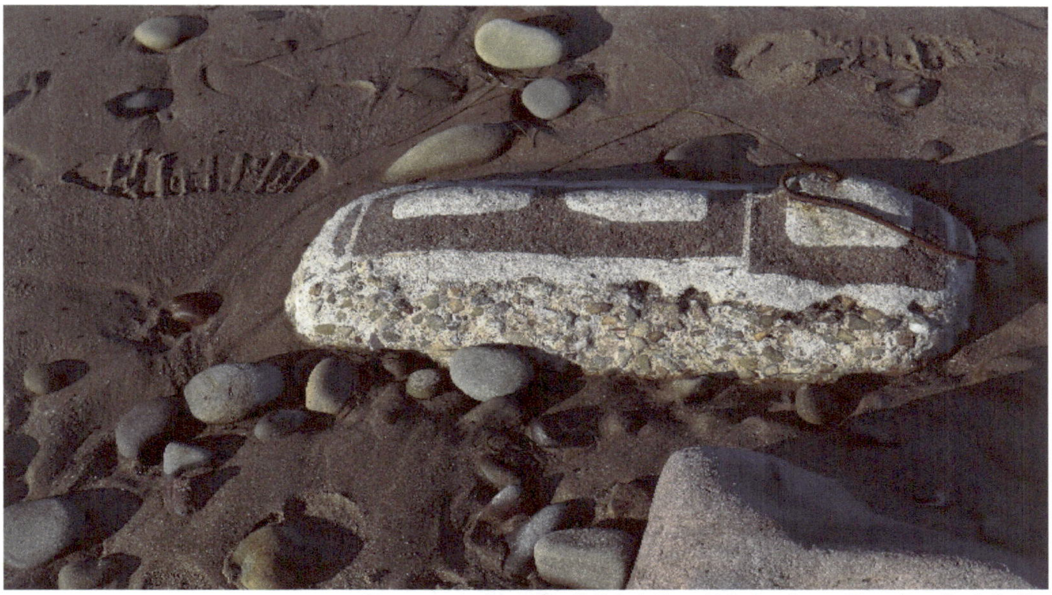

Fly

A brown-skinned girl plays on her grandfather's farm,
chasing her brothers through gardens and ditches,
swerving down, curving back up. They run
to the back porch, proclaim it their "base,"
she turns and heads back, to dip, tumble, laugh.

Bright white teeth against his coal black face,
Grandfather watches from the kitchen window.
He knows his little miss does not have to think
of cotton, or whips, or backs red with blood,
of lost family, of being a commodity.

He watches and beams, he sees the young woman
who will not take flight when it's time to stand firm,
who will not weave in the face of fierce hatred,
who will not laugh when it's time to sit serious,
refusing to budge or leave when commanded.

He sees her at mid–age, eyes blazing, her lesson
that we own our minds, hearts, our mouths,
that we stand firm alone, firmer together,
that some are the head and some the back,
all are the mouth that speak community.

He sees her deathbed, her slight, serene smile,
as she dreams of that window, of his beaming face,
dreams of the girl, running, weaving, and laughing,
dreams of the horses, the carts, cars and planes,
of rockets soaring where she hopes to take wing.

Westside, San Antonio

I.

Here the boys
in their ratty blue jeans
dirty red T–shirts
hold vases
with single red roses
both arms held high like
Mexico City athletes
with vase in each hand
signs that bark
FLOWERS FOR MOTHER'S DAY

II.

Packs of stray dogs
make their way around rusty pick–ups
old sky blue Oldsmobiles
bellow black smoke
here and there
brilliant reds, oranges, ceruleans, yellows
brighter than the morning sun
the family shops stand
gaudy and defiant

Trolley

I saw Frida
on the trolley today
smiling serenely

she stood in back
caressing an imaginary
metal guard rail

Diego in front, sitting,
talking with ghosts
rebellion, redemption

but not for her
doomed to vomit up
the eternal present

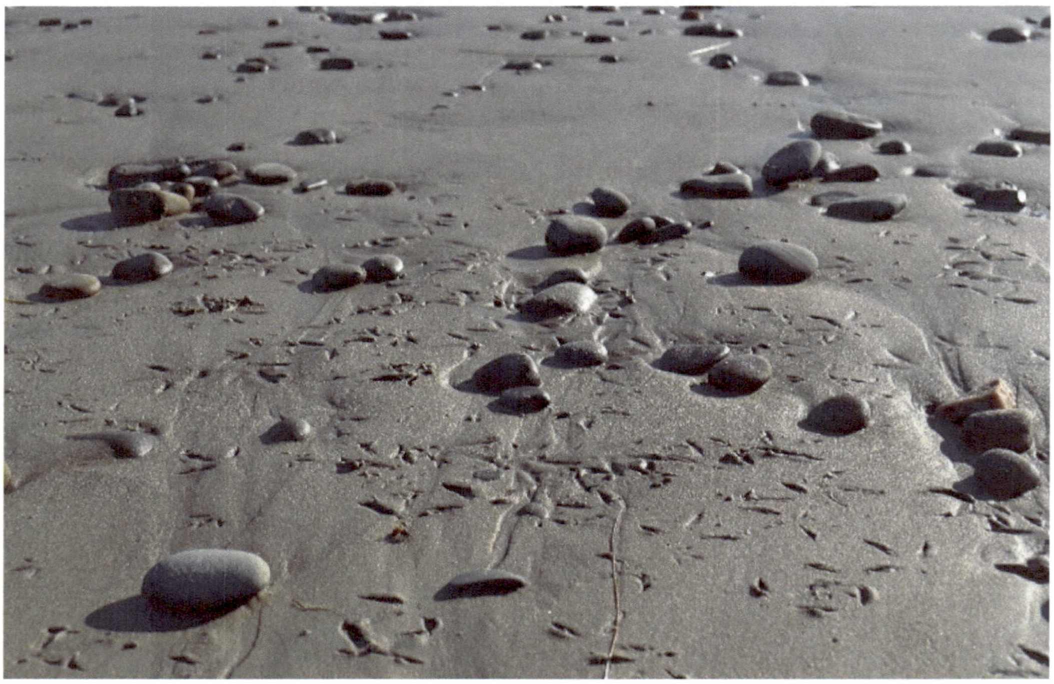

Saturday Prayer

Tonight let us don top hats,
tuxedo jackets made of black
cotton, plugs for our noses,
sun glasses in the dark, dressed
to the nines, our faces shine like
that of a refined corpse.

Let us lewdly dance and swear
in voices of thunder we will pray:
Lurer of the dead, lurid joker
of the cross and the criminal
loan to us this night, coarser minds—
Thoughts formed of smoke and rum.

Loaner of resurrections, Baron Sunday,
speak our names to Saint Vivienne
we who have to spirits gone, now found
at our crossroads, looking to be lead,
Jonesing to be saved by the magic black
caffeinated cure coursing our souls.

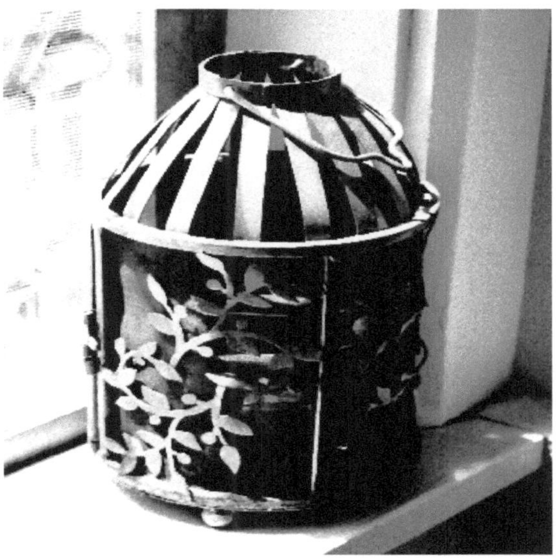

City of Saints

Drogo, patron saint of coffee shops
sips slowly on Sunday morning.
Francis smiles at every dog and owner.
Vivienne, head in hands, curses day—
After daylight. She enjoys her Saturday
nights, jokes Mary Magdalen,
preening and brushing her hair.

People stop by the coffee house, sidle
up to the table, chat up the saintly crew:
How's tricks? Wuzzup? I need a favor. . . .
Unnerved but moved, they smile and nod.

Vitus does his best Brando, while George
tells jokes about driving out snakes.
"Are we there yet?"
And they all laugh, heavenly mirth,
hearing it the millionth time.

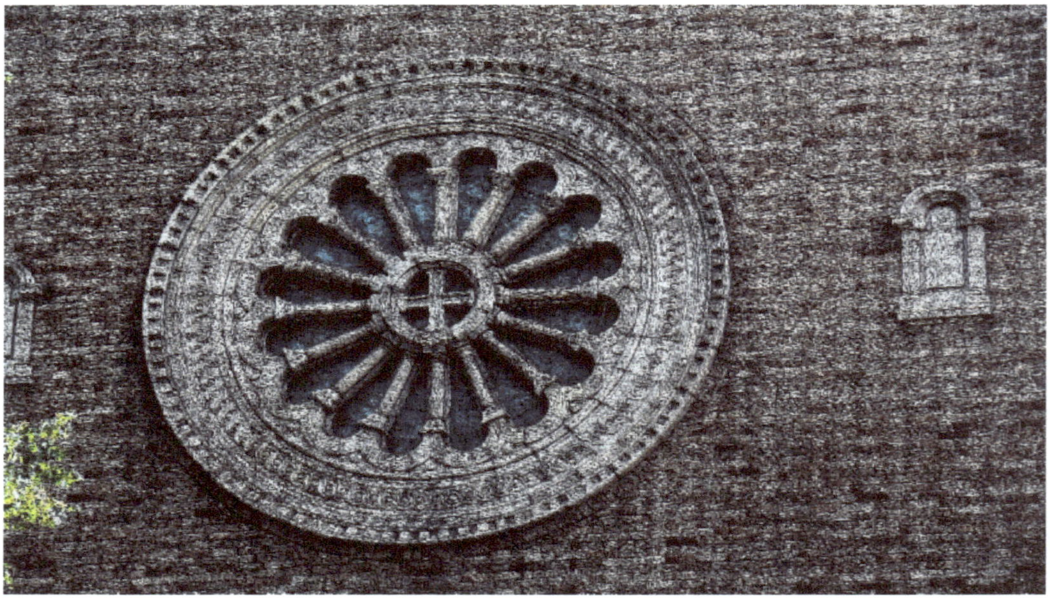

Stasis

Bayou trees stand
unmoved.
No wind looks
to brush their leaves.
Bark like marble,
leaves locked
in amber colored
still skies.

To say
the air stands still
is to look
at a snapshot.
For truth
is to listen
to cricket drone
for music.

H. D. saw heat,
but bayou sky has
weight.
A steel–toed work–boot
twisting downward.
This is the booted State.
Named after monarchy,
after oppression.

And the trees,
and the skies,
and the crickets
take no notice
of the unreal
stillness.

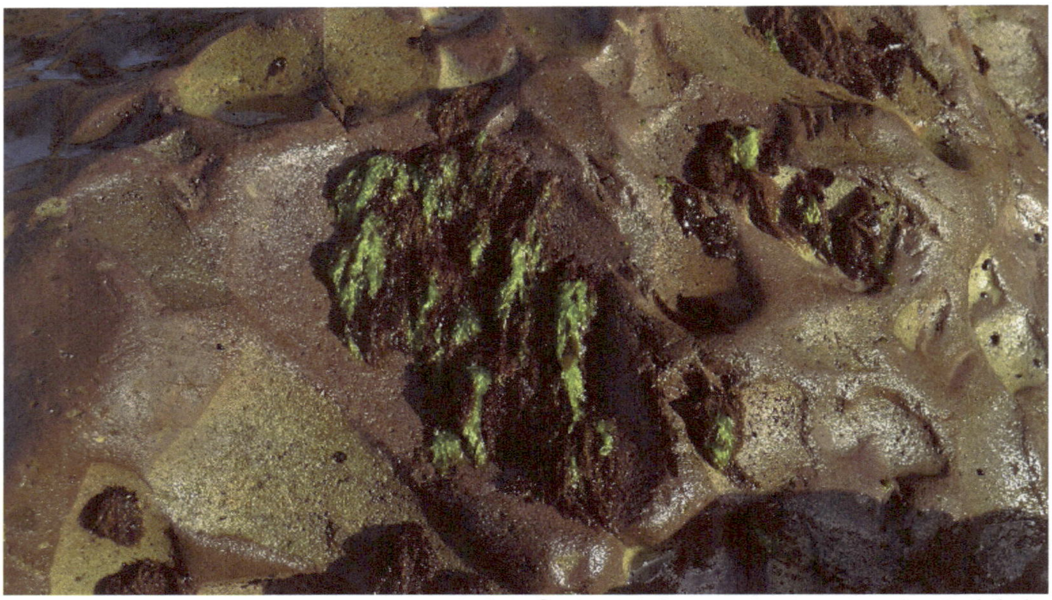

Driving to Work: Westside, San Antonio

I.

He walks by the shelter
His months old beard wire
His pink sweater too small
Minnie Mouse smiling
Hardly noticed by drivers

II.

A white woman weeps
Her head on the shoulder
Of a muscular black man
He holds her tightly
Neither aware of passing traffic
Or gray overcast skies

III.

Warrior camouflaged
In full fatigues
His heavy boots churn
Like the pistons of the passing
Cars he runs alongside
Gaudy painted rundown homes
His painted face expressionless
Running upright,
Holding high his American flag

Flag Day

The summer wind dies
Old Glory falls.
Limp, its contents,
melting, spilled whiteness.
Red waterfalls flow,
while below,
brown children
red to the knees. . . .

But one by one
they reach down,
pick up stars,
place them in pockets,
One by one.

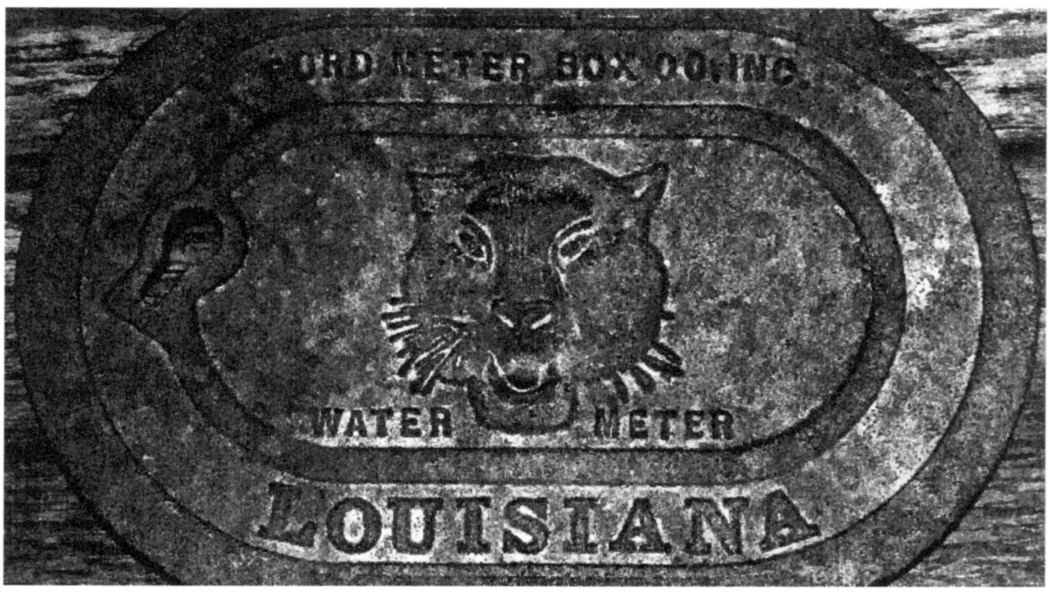

Mia Tierra

It is like the skies burst open:
The raincloud a giant piñata
filled with colors unreal.
Then a crack of thunder
and Saint Anthony smiling,
wielding the winning bat

Colors rain down, surround you.
Some of them brighter than
sun rays, more striking than
lightning.

You cannot help but be struck.
The magic of divine preparation.
Everything becomes artifice—
Time ceases, life calcifies to art.

You cannot grow old.
And nothing can die
when the skies rain such colors.
Sweetness tempers ripeness.
Childhood tempers age.

Saintly artists paint the ceiling.
And you are tainted with beauty
and lost dreams of color, now found.

Tri–Coastal 2: California

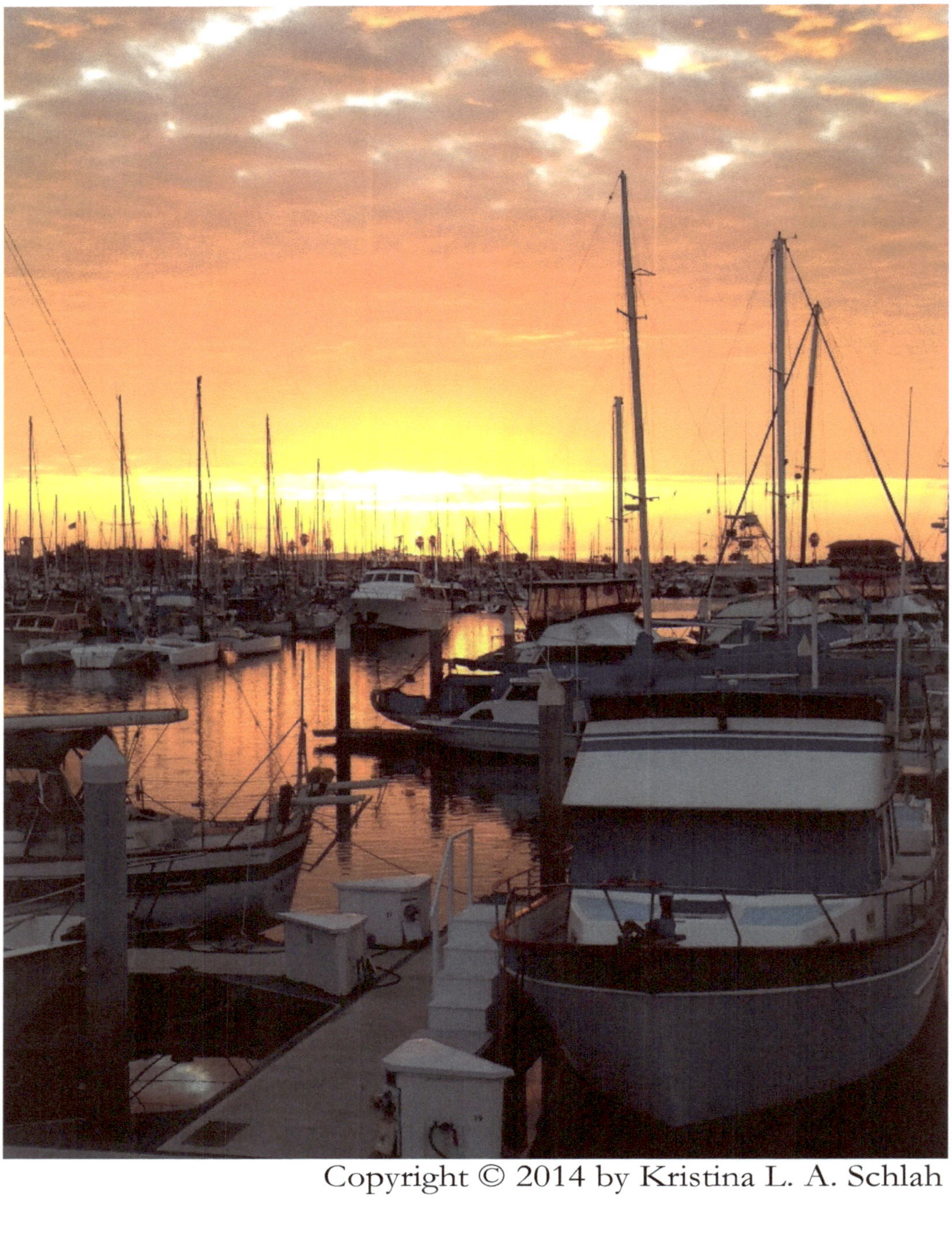

Fire Haikus

I. Tipping the Lantern

And up went the flames,
waltzing late into the night,
five–alarm click track.

II. San Francisco, 1906, Headline

The dynamite walls
failed to form needed firebreaks
to save the city.

III. Substrate

And the flames begin,
rather unexpectedly,
from rag, oil, and match.

IV. Night's Ablazing

The nightclub jazz scene
fills the air with sinewy
smoke from horns on fire.

V. American Darling

Bright, glaring, and red,
you douse cinders, flames, and sparks.
Nothing outshines you.

Music Code #213

I said hey—
And a
        Boom
          Boom
                Boom, Boom, Boom.

Here's a palm tree,
another palm tree,
a date palm tree, and a WHAT?
        WHAT?   WHAT?

Hello, propellers from a wind turbine.
        Hello propellers from a wind turbine.

Those are freak propellers from a wind turbine.
        <Falsetto>Freak propellers from a wind turbine.

And–a–one, two, a–one, two, three, four—
The traffic is bad,
So sing two more:
And–a–one, two—three, four (2x).
        And you're still at stop.

Out of rhythm:

<Three–part harmony>Windshield wipers, windshield wipers, windshield wipers. . . .

<Falsetto to Fade>No rain on your windshields,
        No rain in the reservoirs,
                Here in LA we have a five–year drought.

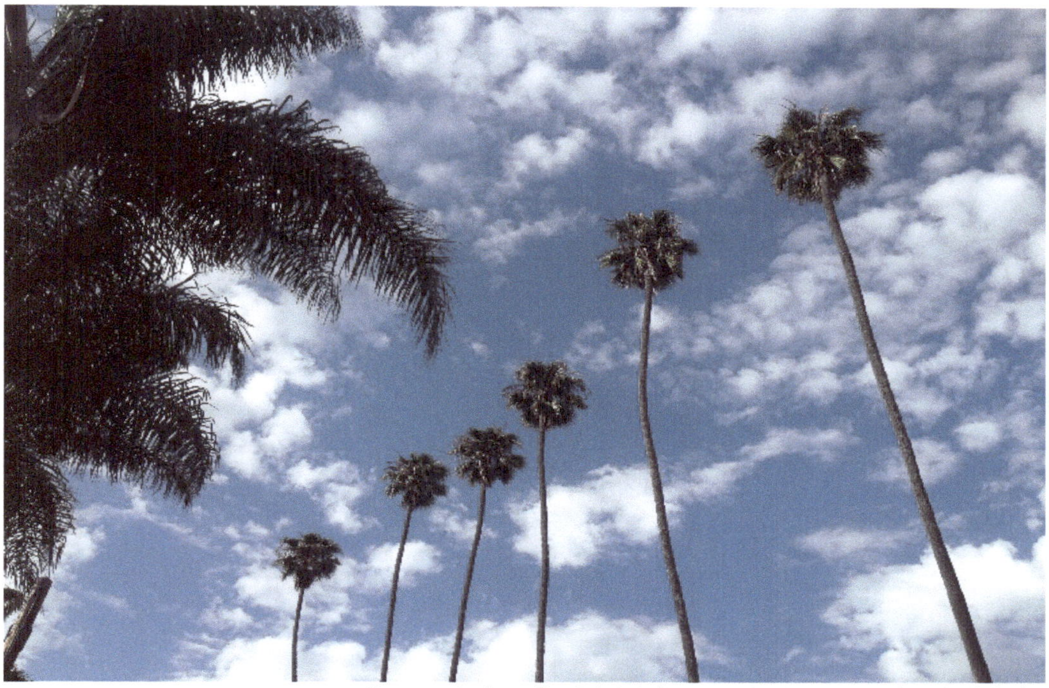

Oh, "Rio"

A Pacific Palisades girl,
a child of the eighties.

Sheila had five pairs of Guess jeans
with matching pairs of jelly shoes.

Her comical outlook on life
was a pink plastic bracelet.

She went to the 3–2–1 Club,
hoping to hear Duran Duran.

Her sweet Irish mother had
spent hundreds on her torn jersey.

She let everyone see her bra—
A right shoulder peek–a–boo strap.

With a green, cellophaned rat tail,
plain Sheila found her difference.

She went to envy skinny girls
at the Santa Monica mall.

She was a Patrick Nagel girl
inside a Mindy Cohn body.

She adored *Flashdance, Fast Times*, and
sang the Buffy overdose song.

A nice, shallow girl of her time,
she never moved a day forward.

"Rio" was her song, but the California sun
melted her cherry ice cream smile.

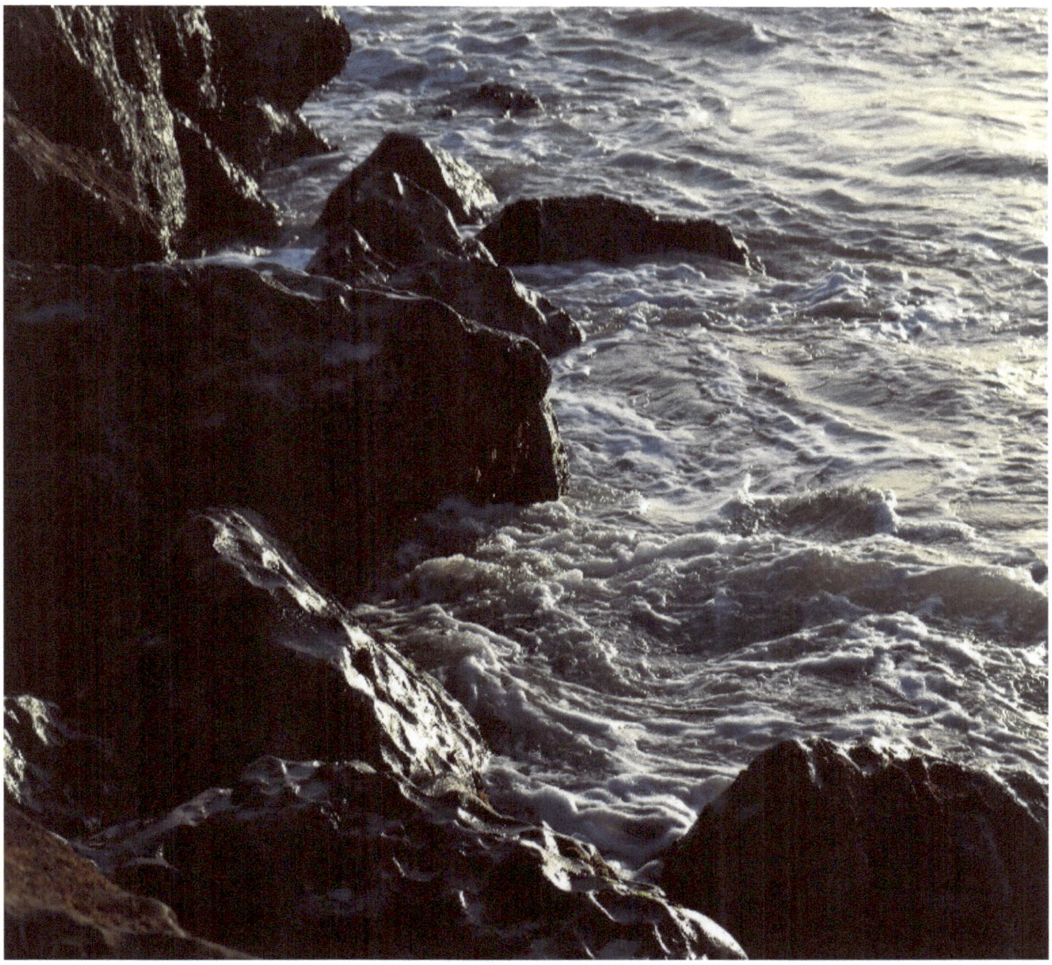

Running Away to the Santa Barbara Public Library

By some long, drawn–out miracle,
the public bus has made its stop.
And I run out of the exit
as quickly as I can.

Maybe the bus driver
won't notice
that I'm a ten year old
who looks like a seven year old.

Across the street
is the Santa Barbara Courthouse.
The library has the same
Old Spanish Days look.

Tiled roofs and stucco,
and murals that would
have fascinated any fan
of cowboys and Indians.

But I drift inside,
First to the literature section
to read a page
written by Professor Huxley.

I browse the LPs and art books,
find a place in
the Children's area,
where I don't look alone.

It isn't a wasted
day after all,
and I wish that every day
could be this productive.

This was in the days
when the sweet smell of musty books
was still a delight
to a kid like me.

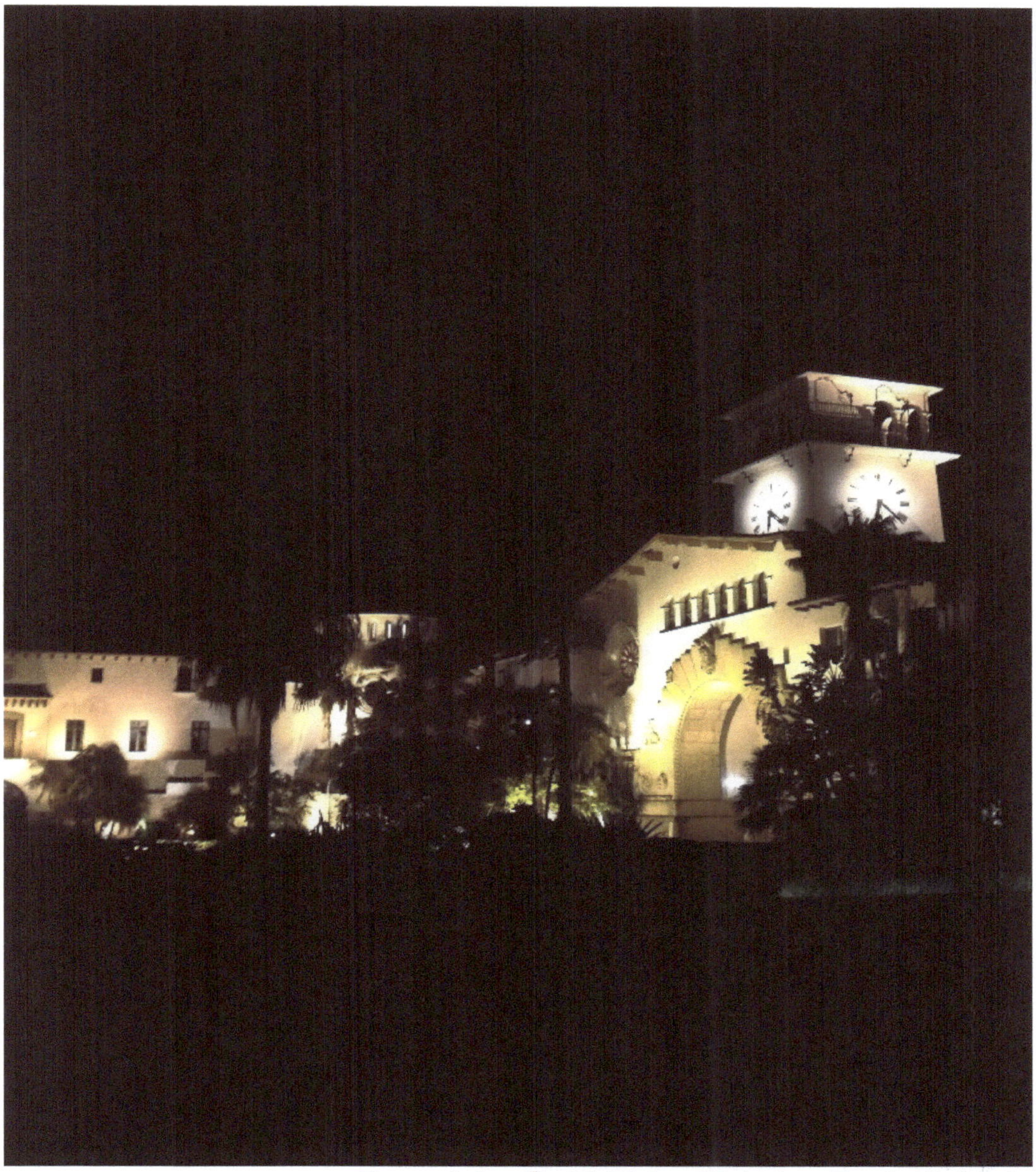

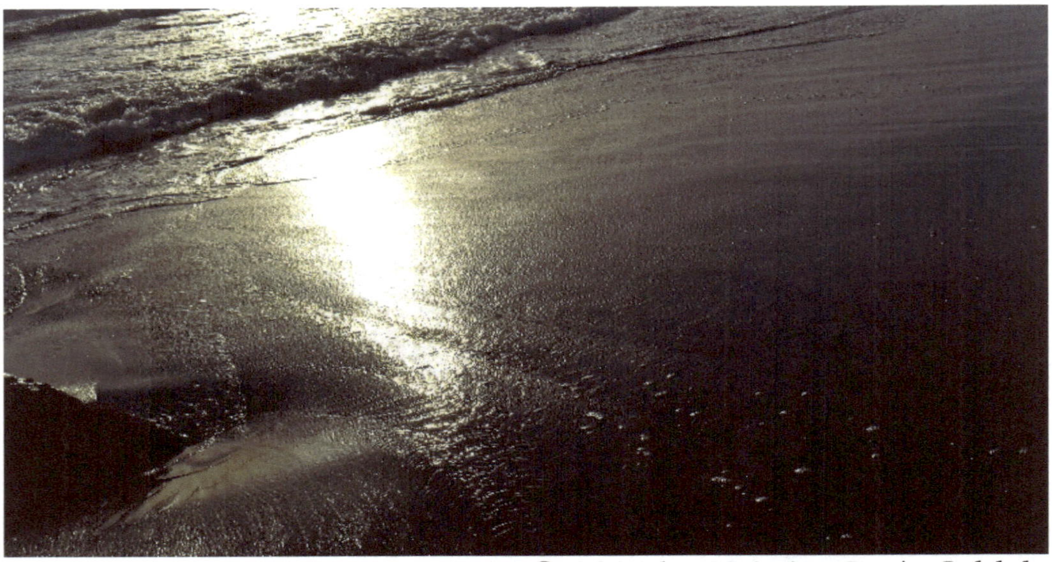

Beach Buds

The beach sand flows
Between my toes
Gulls hang in the sky
Whitewash approaches
Then it goes
Waving goodbye

We smile like the sun
As ocean foam rises
Crashes into the pier
Our lungs filled with
The breath of mist with
The here and now

We huddle like gulls
Chasing crumbs on a beach
Our breath now filled with
The mist of our smokes
That we pass along to friends
Silent as the sunset

Manic Sue

One day, Manic Sue
went to the Copper Teapot
to smear her shit
all over their bathroom walls.
And that was just
her morning.

Needless to say,
she was not
asked back
to the establishment.

Manic Sue took herself
further downtown
that day
for other adventures.
For Santa Barbara had a heart
for people like Manic Sue.

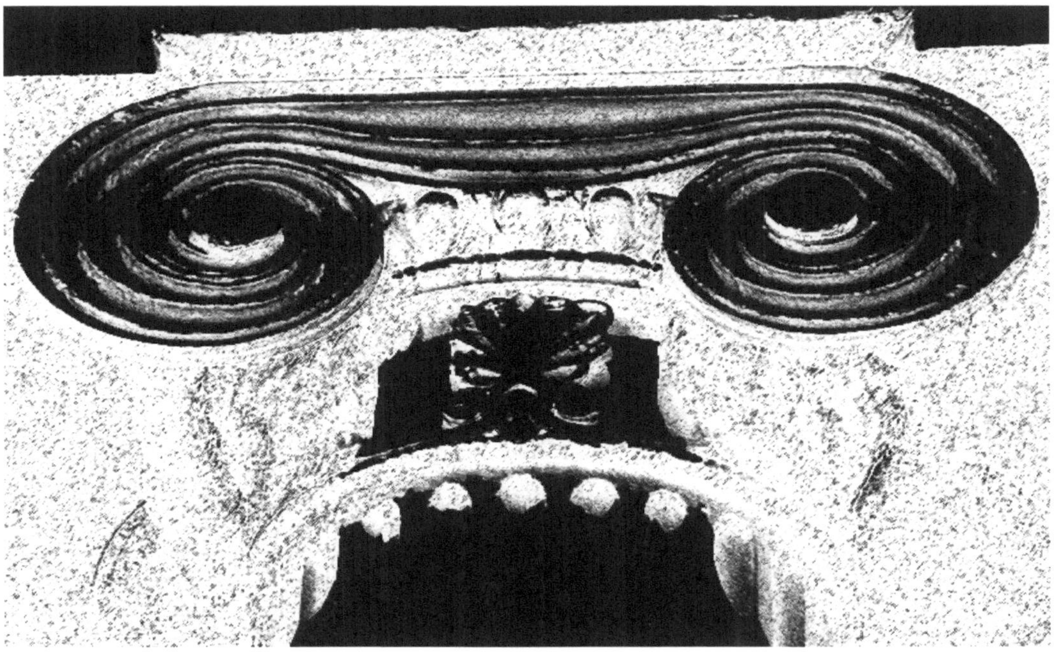

The Stoner Mirror

I need a blue mirror
for tripping,
especially on days
or nights
when I find friends
and we smoke M.

My parents have no clue
what the blue mirror
is all about.

They think
it's a weird teenage thing,
like my
Mad Magazine paperbacks
or my
Weird Al record collection.

I like
that the blue mirror
can take me places—
like the Valley or Venice Beach.

I'm not just
some nobody
in a flannel shirt
with dreams
of getting out of here—
and pizza.

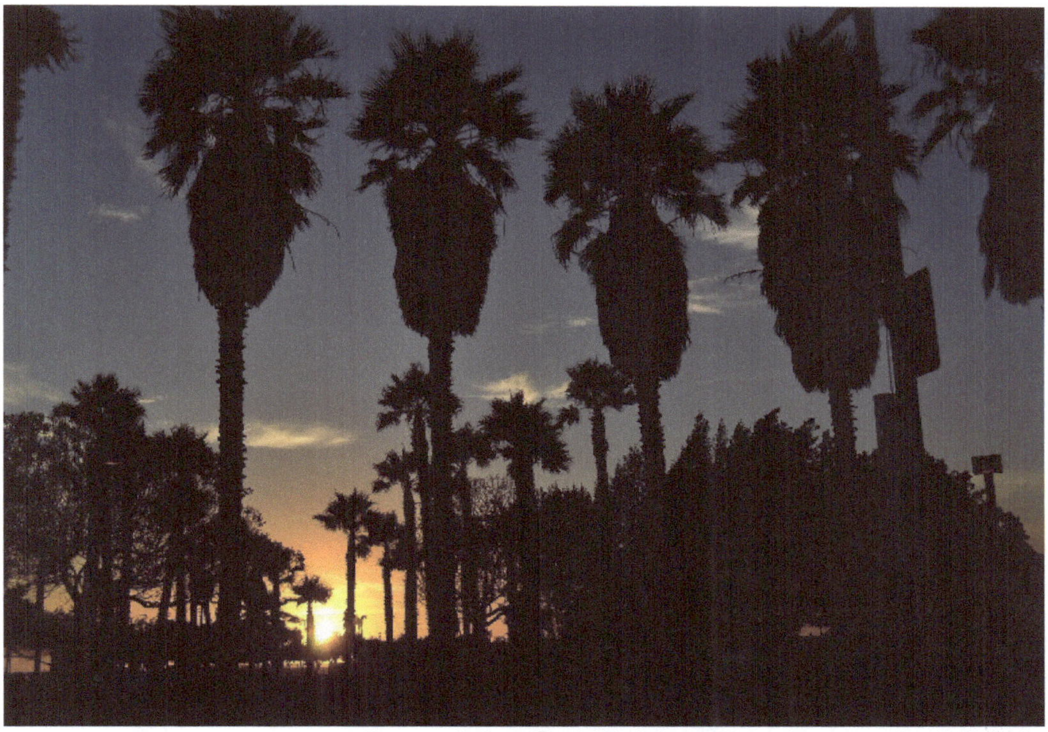

Tri–Coastal III: Massachusetts

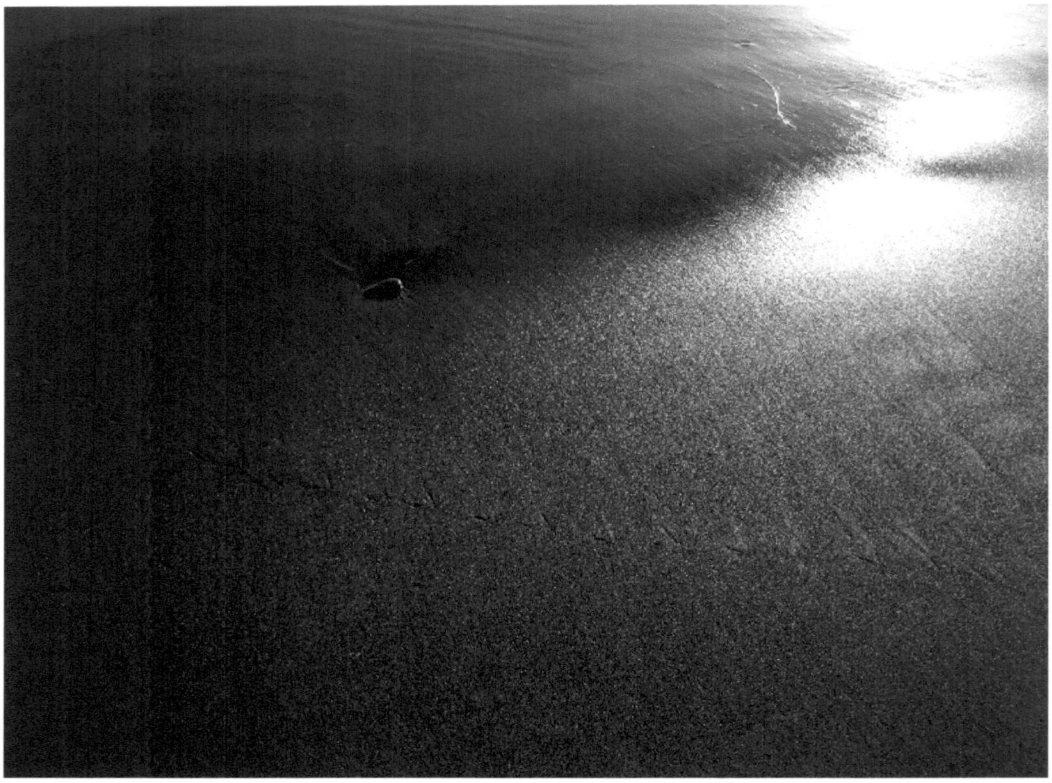

Valley Lightning

The first thing that struck me was
the lack of rain, the dearth of the
deluge that you see along the Gulf
where rain is that insistent brother–in–law
who splashes into rooms like a belly–flopper,
demands attention's center of every parade
Gulf Coast rain won't be ignored
It won't let up, it won't go away
and everything becomes rain
cars turn into pirogues,
shoes into boots,
land into swamp

Nothing so mundane is the rain
that greets the valley, rather it
is the family manic–depressive, the sister,
or brother, or great–nephew who arrives
in a gray mist, a fog, an oppressive,
constant threat of cloudburst that waits
and waits, and waits, but instantly hits
with an impressive array of growls,
and groans, and streaks of moments so
electric as to make Armageddon into art
nothing changes once it passes
sunshine to sunshine,
dirt to dirt.

But you will remember that you were marked
at that moment, and knew myth, and power,
and what fear had to be, and you internalized
beyond the word, the essence of impressive

Snow Globe World

The ice couch on the screened in porch
cars turned into mounds of snow
iced branches and twigs, with no birds
and icicles ten feet long hanging from
the neighbor's roof; this snow globe world
of single–digit cold wants to freeze the spirit
and trap the body inside a heat filled house
but there is something magical about the white
covered streets filled with child–like adults
even the woman on cross–country snow skis
shows no sign of toil; the world has become
fun again, just to walk through the icy pathways
reminds us that walking should be precarious,
an adventure waiting to unfold itself anew
every time we take the same well–worn path
layered up, we walk along and smile at each other
because we both have rediscovered something
once lost, or misplaced so deep inside that every
snowplow in the county would admit defeat
and head for the warmth of its garage home.
But we pass the woman walking her prancing collie
none of us feeling the bone–chill of the air
it is winter, and soon we will wish for spring
its colors a match for the beauty of solid white,
but for now, we wave and exchange smiles, and
hurriedly place our hands back in our pockets.

Richard the Poet at 3 AM

In the middle of a death–still, snowy night,
past November's falling leaves,
and decaying horse chestnuts,
Richard the poet dances by himself
on the Smith College campus
while future women leaders of the world
are sound asleep.

As if related to Gypsy Boots,
or a character from a Dr. Seuss book,
he pony–steps to music
in his head,
swinging
his knee–long knitted hat's
tiny pom–pom.

If madness and beauty
can have such an exchange,
it is here,
in the middle of a snowstorm,
pom–pom singing,
and death–evading—
joyous.

Red traffic lights flash nearby,
already checked–out for the night,
but Richard the poet
has not only checked in;
he is now
the official emcee
of his own private rave.

Underneath a New England Trestle

One would never expect
a red tiki mask
placed underneath a New England Trestle.

An outer–space troll,
his billy goats roll over him,
carrying tanks of chemicals and coal.

He stares with gold and black eyes
down at unsuspecting walkers,
who never look up.

A long, lost scavenger hunt prize,
placed carefully for discovery,
but his mystery went unsolved.

In the timeless winter,
he is especially out of his element,
witnessing snow, sleep, and death.

He stands out like a Currier and Ives house
in the middle of a white landscape,
but nobody looks up when it's cold.

Maybe he curses passersby,
but more likely the poor thing is cursed,
always looking, always watching.

In his last life,
he enjoyed fire and the beach,
but he crossed someone powerful.

So now, he's a trestle tiki,
in a small New England town,
where he wishes people would just look up.

The Fireflies

They do little for the world,
lighting up,
visible then invisible,
wandering from place to place:
Dante's lovers;
insect Bohemians.

The darker the night,
the brighter they burn.
But they have no idea
they are part of a show.
Onlookers dread their
disappearance.

Aimless yet desirable,
they are forgiven.
These days everyone understands
why they ignore the world,
oblivious to their surroundings,
flying, flying, flying. . . .

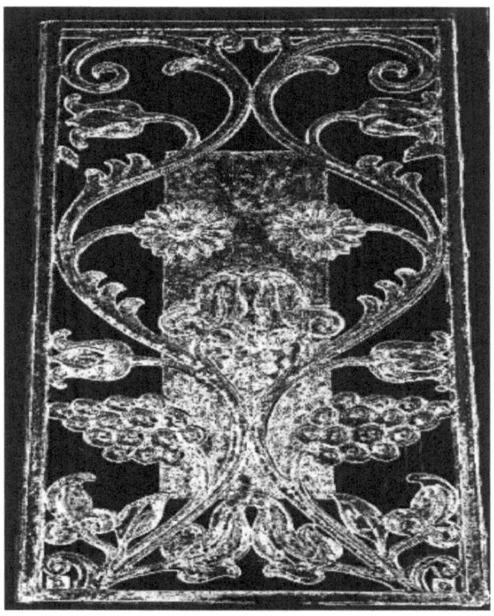

Crochet Shade Pull

You are from another time.
The dorms don't need you anymore
and no more orders will be made
to replace you.

Not that the art of making you is lost;
and not that you are no longer useful.
Your purpose has been simply
ignored into obscurity.

So what if you
aided the sleep of young Kelly,
eased Sarah's reading, or
spared Eleanor from skin cancer.

You belong in an old house
with antimacassars,
acorn–shaped stair posts,
and dumbwaiters.

I now stare at you from outside
my old dorm window.
I was the only one
who ever thought of you.

Will you be disposed
with your accompanying shade?
Or will a student unravel you
for her newest knitting project?

You have aged perfectly.
All the oils
from young women's hands
didn't soil your ecru.

Now I can’t really keep you,
and I measure my years
by walking by
just to see if you are still there.

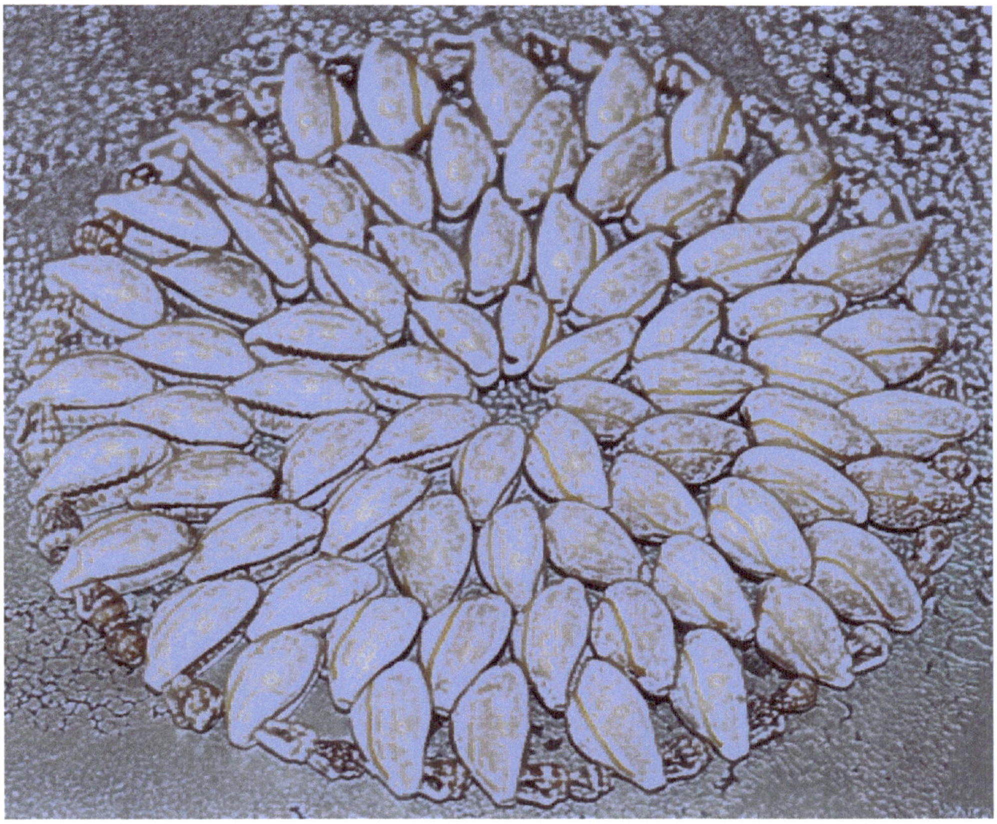

Musical Code #413

Boom, boom, boom, boom,
ch . . . ch . . . ch . . .
ch. . . .
snappity
snappity
snappity
snappity.
Da da da doooooooo
Da da da
doooooooo.

<<insert Booker T. organ here>>
crash, craSH, CraSH, CRASH.
Dr–oh–
oh–oh–oh–oh–
oh–oh–oh . . .
oh–oh–oh–oh–oh–nnnnnnnnnnnnnnnnne.

One (clap) two (clap) three (clap) four (clap).
<<needs more bass>>
One (clap) two (clap) three (clap) four (clap).
chachachacha chachachacha
o
d
n
a
s
s
i
l
g
<<ascending>>

Take it down.
Take it down.
Take it down.
Turn it down.

Boom–clip–clip, Boom–clip–clip, Boom–clip–clip, and break.
Pass the God–damned butter, clap–clap.

And–a–Boom, boom, boom, boom,
And–a–Boom, boom, boom, boom.
Sss, sss, sss, sss.
And—a–Boom, boom, boom, boom,
and–a–Boom, boom, boom, boom. <<4x and fade>>

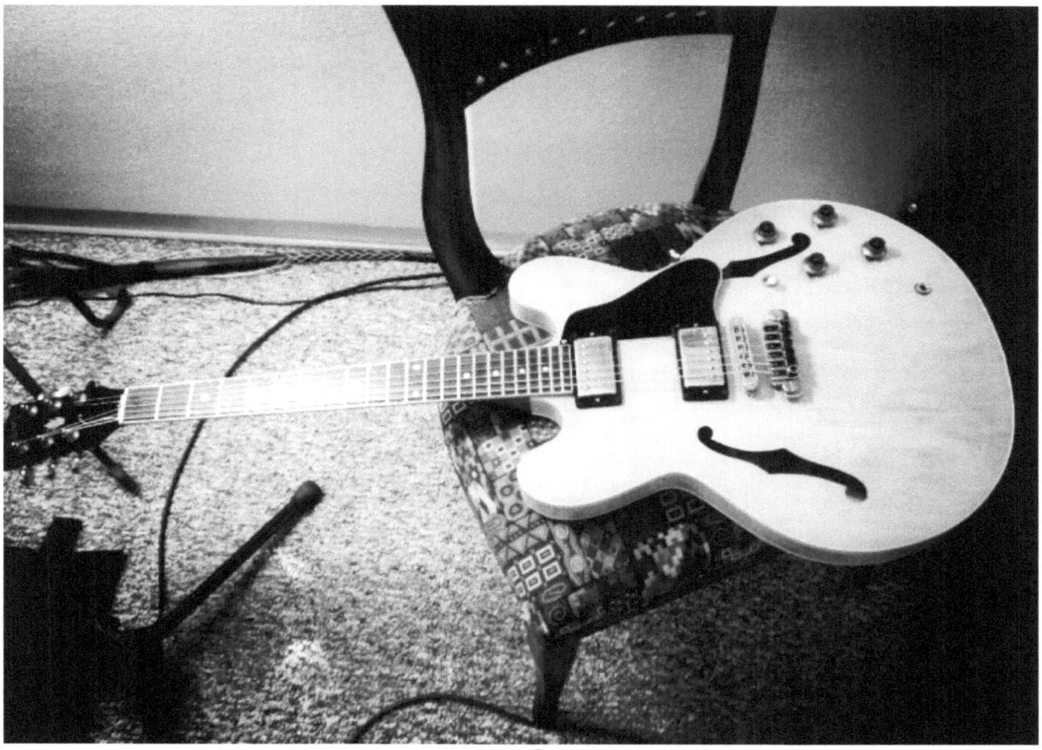

Antique Store Windows

Set up like Norman Rockwell paintings,
they remind us that there's no time machine.
But rather jumbled pieces that
define many times,
several houses,
and lives gone past.

The warm light
from a Chinese lamp
invites everyone to look in.
Who cares that
there's no telling
of a collective when?

What a curse to be a vintage object.
The child's sled or uke would never reside
next to Wedgewood china or a twill pen.
The Groucho Marx drawing
never propped against the
Nutting chairs.

The warm light
from a Chinese lamp
invites everyone to look in.
Who cares that
there's no telling
of a collective when?

It beats the fluorescence
of other places.
Fluorescence is a conspiracy,
an effort to make you move away.
You know your home
is where the warm light glows.

The warm light
from a Chinese lamp
invites everyone to look in.
Who cares that
there's no telling
of a collective when?

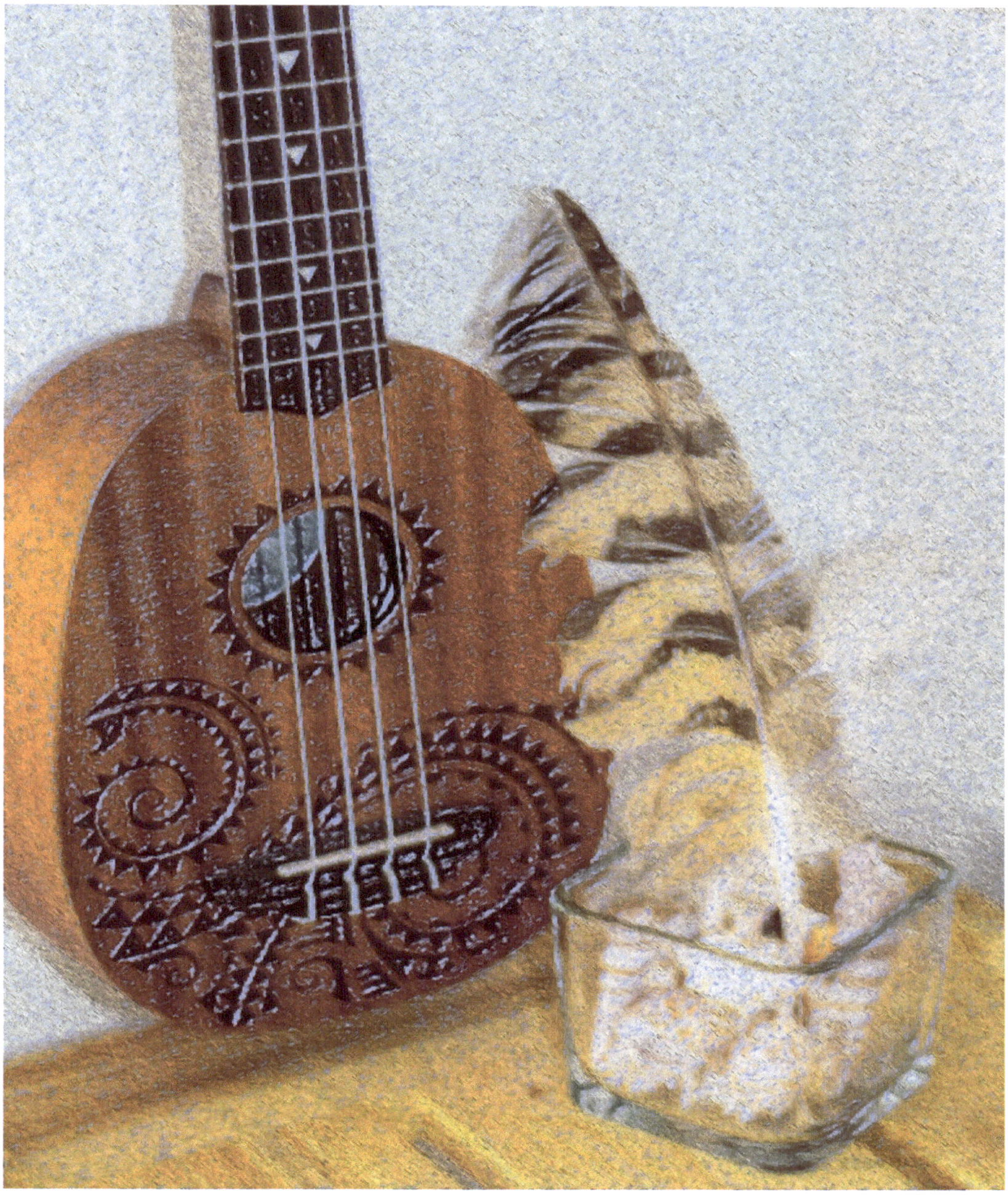

Other Poems

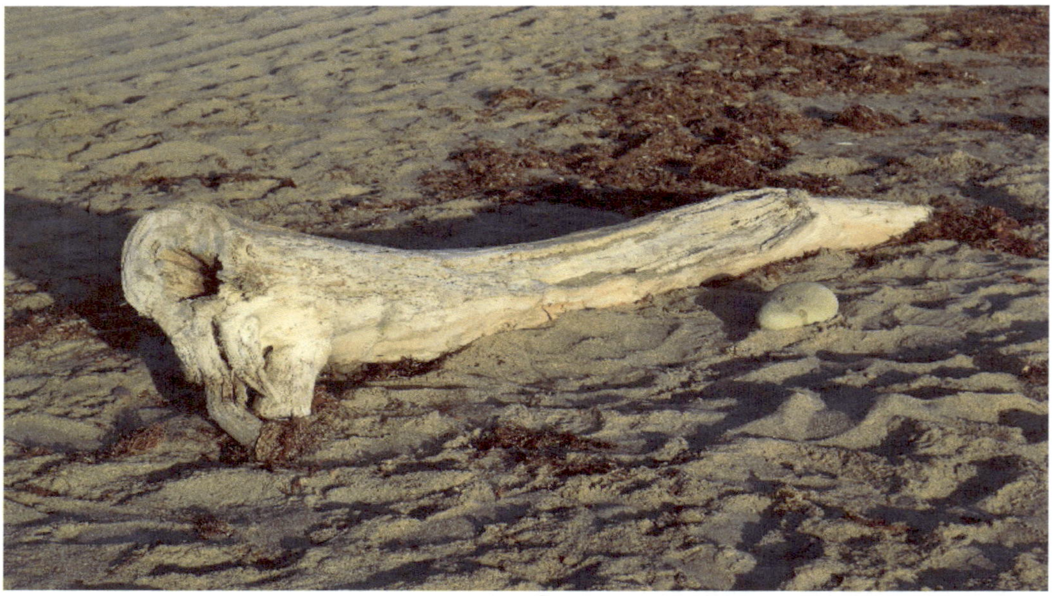

Ivory Tower

You cannot be touched.
You are too rich,
too powerful,
know where the skeletons are buried,
buried the skeletons yourself.

Those under your command
fear losing their jobs,
fail to speak out,
take the abuse you dole out to them.
Some abusing others
to make you look the other way.

Threats are nothing to
someone who cannot be touched.
Promises of lawsuits,
forcing disclosure,
wishing to unionize—
meaningless, un–materialized.

When challenged,
you fire back:
You oust,
you restructure,
you belittle,
you destroy.

A dime a dozen,
you leap
from one ivory tower
to the next.
Everyone knows
It's your five–year plan.

RIP, university.

RIP, college.
RIP, education
RIP, greater good.
Higher learning now
re–made in your image;
college reimagined as
an empty, corporate vessel.

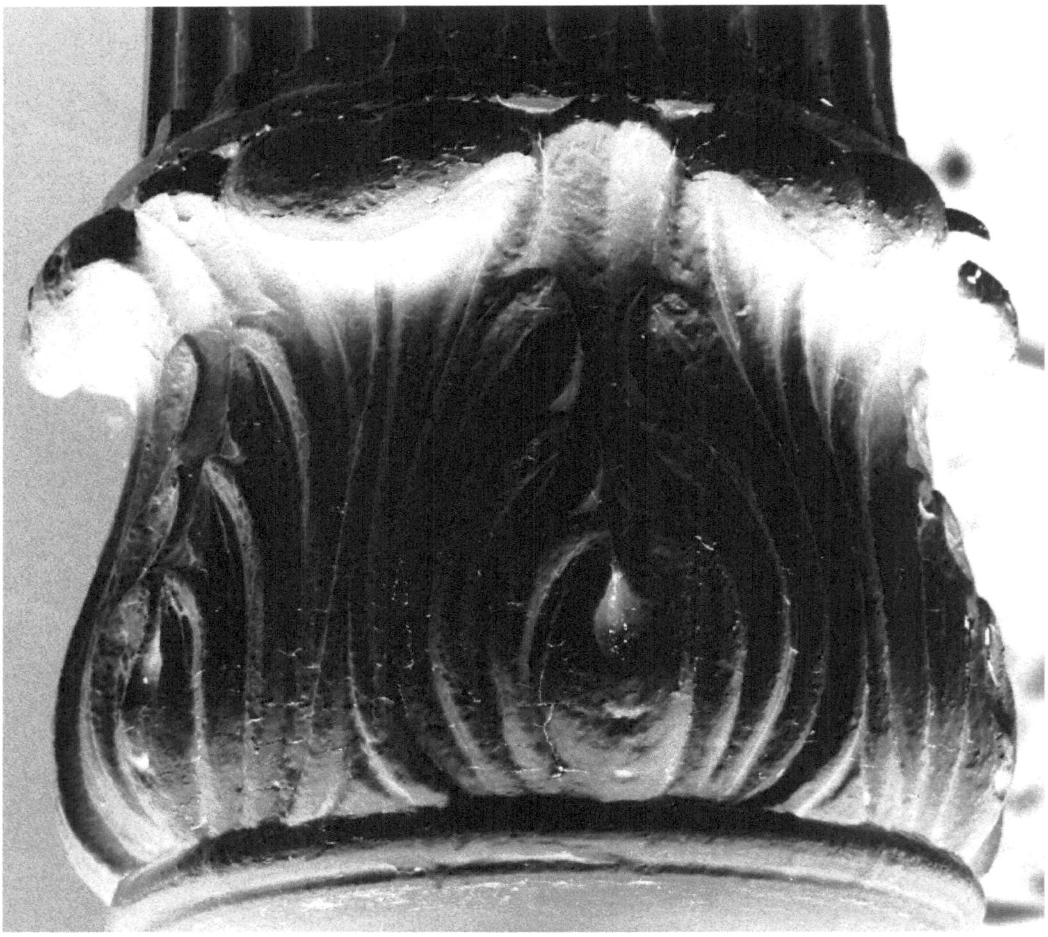

Carabo–Cone Method: Bass Clef with Defiance

to learn to
clef read
F- all
an the don't
of bass try
shape notes
to the in a to
dance m stop
I u me.
S
i
c
a
l
p
i
e
c
e
.

Songs from a Glass Church

Wafting—
music, but not so steadily the
words,
and circles become broken.

Feeling
The
Spirit
involves chasing a d r i f t i n g s o u l.

The "Old One Hundredth"
has found a loosened, new accord.

If this is North,
Then the "Star of the East"
has traveled West.

Flying swift(ly) around us,

These
wheels
of
time
have flown,
have flown,
in fuguing—
circles of
their own.

These songs,
fragmented,
like the church's outermost walls.

The earth
shall soon
d i s so l v e

like s n o w.

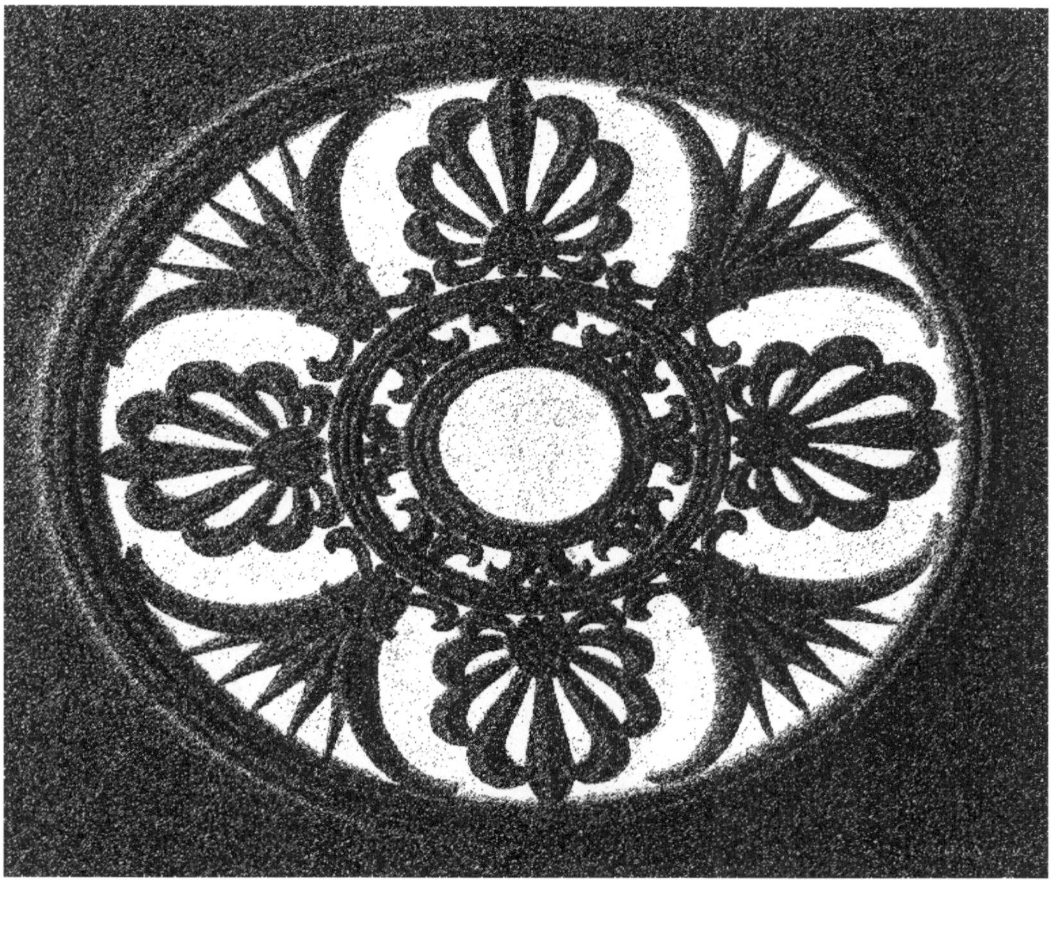

Predator

Dear Ex–Student of Mine,

Though years have passed,
I thought I'd remind you,
here in public,
at just the right time,
that not all my colleagues
supported your work.

It seems to me
that in your current career
you would not like it
for information like this
to get out there,
yet here I write it.

What I won't write
are facts
like I'm still bat–shit crazy,
or I had student lovers of my own,
or I feared approaching you,
but hinted at my crush all the time.

Never mind
the fact
I use people,
can't hold a position,
offend nearly everyone
I know.

Every part of my brilliant mind,
is now a predictable,
mostly lustful,
semblance of intellectual effort.

And through your own success,
I can still stalk you.

I now want to teach you again,
even though I failed you.

—D.

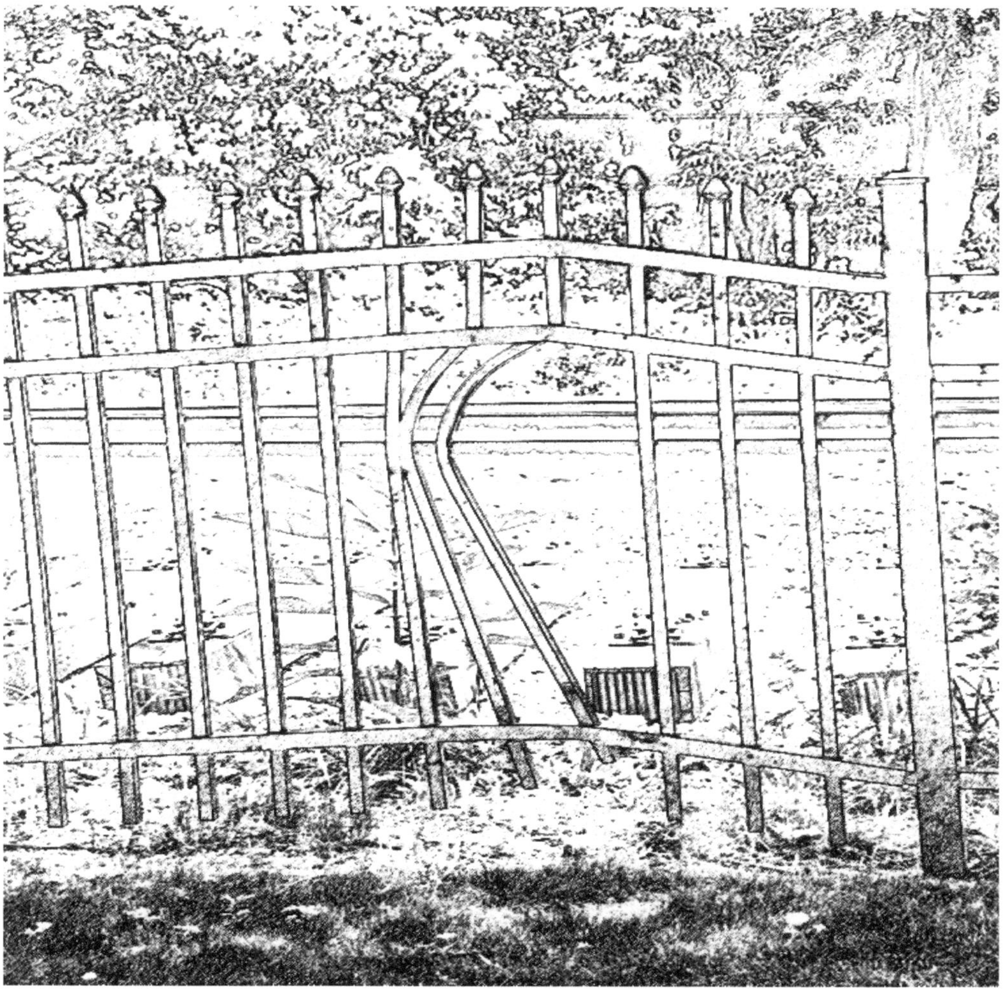

Ghosts on Earth

My mom believed that she had seen ghosts.
I was always open to the idea.

So, when she told me about seeing her mother waving in the window,
I believed her.

I looked forward to hearing her stories of seeing a headmaster from 100 years ago,
using the closet to hang up his trench coat.

The old Licking Water School apartment wafted of ghost perfume—
she described it as a lovely scent that was much like a single floribunda.

When ghosts presented themselves to her,
she'd find out as much as she could about them at Forbes library.

Her typical, predictable, explanation was unfinished business,
but she couldn't help but notice their curiosity in us.

Louise lived in our townhouse and found her place
to be such a comfortable, old shoe that she couldn't leave.

Her stepmother's father just wanted to climb the stairs,
and so he did, and nothing more.

After my mom died,
I didn't want to believe in ghosts anymore.

I could not bear to have her watch me
give her items away or see me cry as often as I did.

I like to think that she is elsewhere, at least for a while,
where she can visit other people and let time become a lost concept.

It would be much better for her to travel than to stay attached to a single place,
unless she wants to make friends with strangers.

Don't worry. She's friendly and she just doesn't want to be alone.
And she loves to watch people.

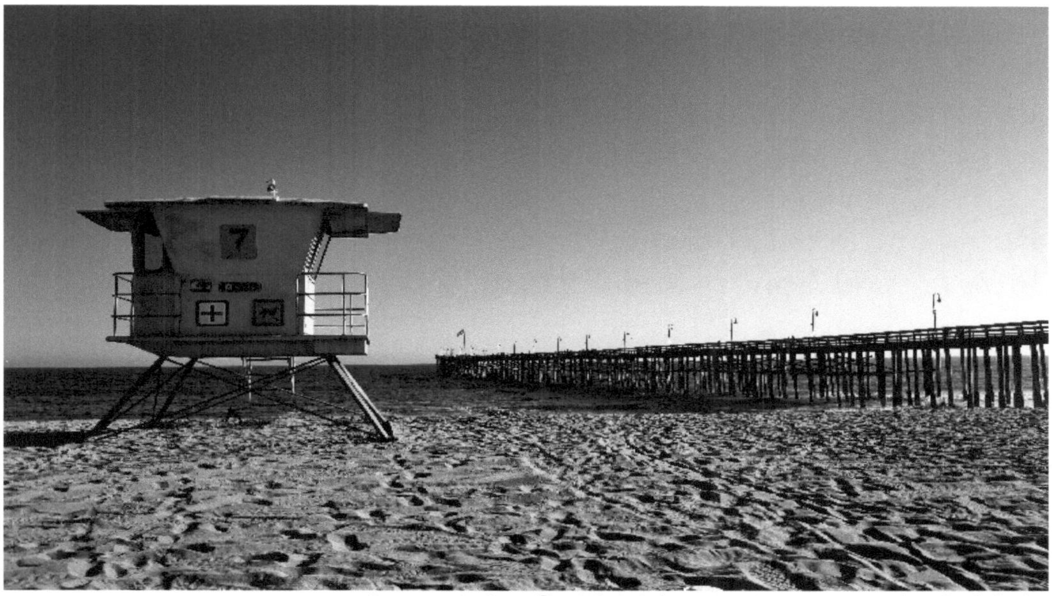

Laurels

The accolades on the wall
make their owner stand so tall.

And gathering such awards
leads our hero to springboards.

Dust collectors, some small plaques,
and more trophies with cash whacks.

Grants displaying his success
gain attention from the press.

That article won a prize,
brought his career to a rise.

From writing a short chapter,
to pen some books thereafter.

Recognition is his name.
He's earned honors and acclaim.

Time's drudgery to find more.
There he is: The laurels whore.

The Final Cut

When it was over, you held out the knife.
You were gloating,
the portrait of an artist of her own pain.

Your words, intended as blades,
their effect, more serrated
than sharp.

Then you showed me gifts,
self–inflicted items
bought to placate your
          self–hate.

But I thought,
better to spoil yourself
than cut yourself.

Too many days I relived
the first day
you told me,
"They held a knife to me.
One of them brought it down.
To my genitals. They
threatened to cut me.
I was so scared
being only twelve."

I was silent then.
But seeds were sown.

Tonight, when you held out your arm
I saw the new blossoms—
A garden of crimson twigs

over older weeds
going magenta to brown.

Deadhead them—
Their bloom will fade,
they will wither and fall:

Petal
by petal
by petal.

But you gather them up,
you press them to fill
the pages of memory.

I dreamt a tub of warm water—
You
floating among petals,
dyeing.
A scarlet ring.

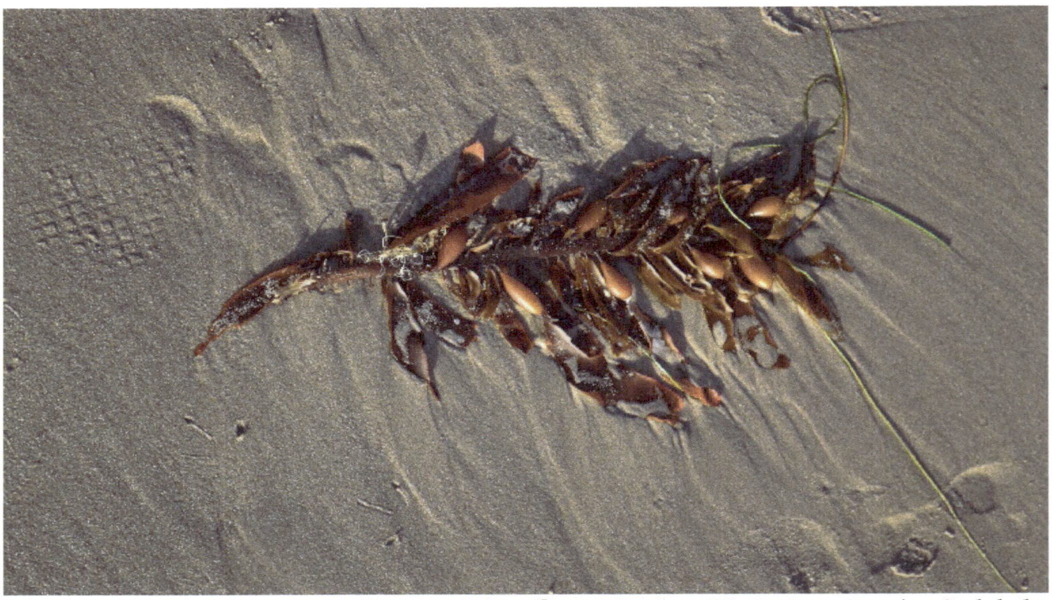

Saturday Night, 1962

He stares at the fives, ones, quarters
enveloped by smoke, his eyes
slide back and forth, counting.
The four men bang cards at a table.
Domestic goddess on the silver screen,
Laura Petrie stands in the kitchen.

My mother sits and chuckles to herself.
Children gathered around. They half
listen to the men talk jobs and bosses.
She breathes easily, the haze unable
to choke her earned contentment.

My father questions his counts, curses
his luck, asks for coffee, spreads a new hand.
He concentrates harder.

She thinks
about cigarette butts, empty cups,
sticky beer cans and dirty glasses,
pots of beans, rices, breads, gumbos.
Then ironing shirts, folding towels, cleaning
rooms, about more children, more
mouths wrapped around needs and wants.

Laura stutters, "Oh Rob" on cue, and cans
of laughter erupt. The children cackle.
Silently, my mother goes to the cupboard.

Death Bed

"He could move like James Brown,"
my mother would say, recalling
the boy sliding across her floor.

I remember music.
He squats harmonica–happy,
a private tune to fill the void.
Skidrow the Scottie howling
in dog–harmony delight.

I still see him grinning,
rolling his smokes,
his private joke whizzing
over young heads that were unacquainted
with "Monsieur Zigzag."

And in smoke filled rooms,
the impossible shots he sank,
a cue stick geometry class of
lines, angles, backspin, speed.

We try to forget the dying man—
A skin–covered child skeleton,
eyes wide with cancer–fear,
veins pumping morphine,
12 minute intervals.

We stayed in turns, waiting.
We talked, eyes downcast, death
weighing every word,
each alone, we all jones
for the morphine of memory.

Random Acts Of

metallic ghosts
stand
in a fog of dust
debris
charred dreams
piles
where once stood
towers

divine
aspirations
concretized
not beautiful, but
wondrous
the human spirit
elevated

phantom like
white
muscle strained
humanity
tear–stained
eyes

visions of
glory
soot caked
tears
faces, lined with
defiance
they trudge
forward

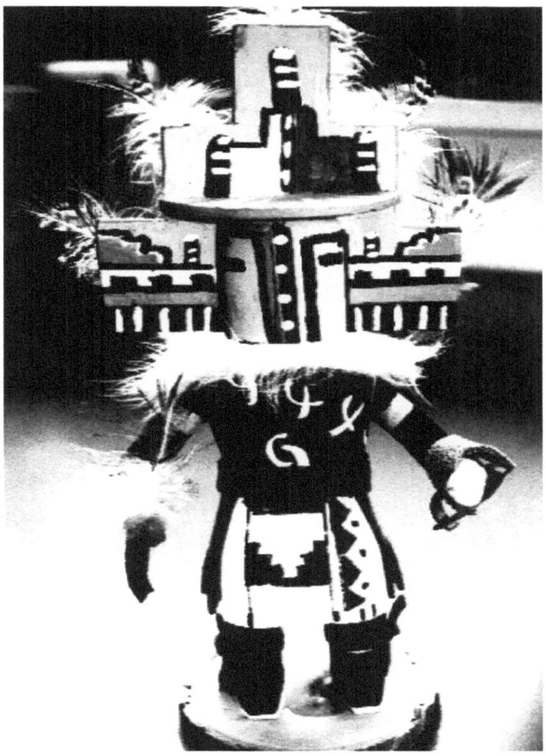

Alkylholics Anonymous

warm, dizzy, sense of
love
rather
relaxation
into the recreational
into the sexual
into the pleasurable

come to popper
is what he said
bring your hardware
he joked
get your 66 kicks and dis-
cover your quick-

Hi–Ho Silver

what a rush
like he was less un-
reactive, like he could be-
long to the func-
tional group
sudden
involuntary
just relax

is what his muscles said

flowers bloom from
glass seeds
yellow blossoms begging
to be inhaled
a cracking
a popping
a rebirth into

pleasure
a new you-
phoria
smoother
more in-
tense or-

chasm

eyes dilate blood flow heart free dilate sex as some-
thing
else
artifice
arteries

lapse momentary
recovery
to irony
a cure for his poisons
a cleaner for his viewing
pleasure

but to irony
his burned skin
his blurred vision

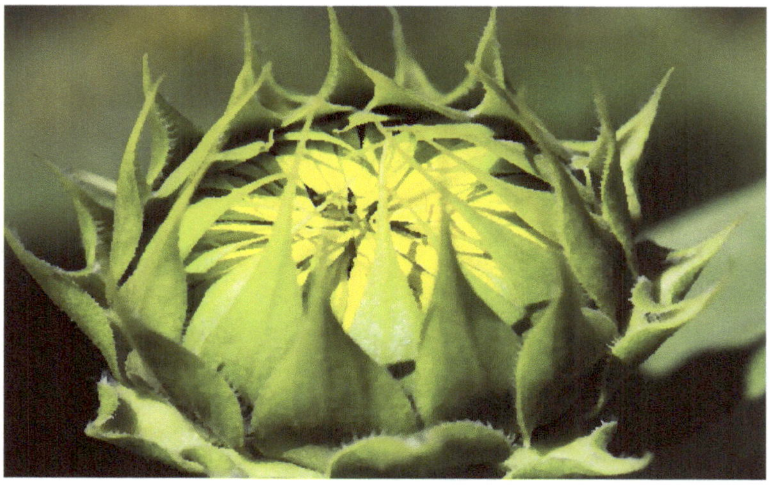

Amnesiac

I.

the first sound was inarticulate buzzing,
musical droning, oracular chanting of
a slow, steady melody, while gently
the keys to his emotions were fingered

he slowly opened his fists, digits spreading
to baby blue hues beyond his reaching,
the liquid world escaped his grasping,
pushed back, until ripples of white blinded

the first color was white, like
driving through fog, where
one can see, at best
ahead a few feet, yet
one always knows
the inevitability of destination

the second color was black
and it created life, outlines
and shadows:
buildings. trees. houses. people.

A cacophony of gray.

She laughs a hearty laugh
pours him a beer on tap
winks, and says, "man
is the animal that makes himself"
amused as she turns her back,
mumbles "trailing clouds of glory"

II.
he should have splashed like a raindrop
falling from the clouds, but balloon–like,
he got twisted into shapes by branches
barely discernable human form, folded
up on himself, he waited and rested,
nursing his bruises until ordered to move
a puppet with wrists and knees strung
his head was left hanging with each lift

he bobbed as he moved, lifting and falling
an awkward motion, his arms useless flapping
lifted up, dropped again, but always inching
forward, walking almost on his knees, scraping
the ground, sometimes his forehead touching,
stumbling ahead, he was lead to the

Reflection:

sadness is a hue beyond blue
spirit darkening to purple shades
red thoughts ooze from the scalp
flowing downward to the chin
to meet lips, where words sit

Reflection:

black as charcoal on canvas

eyes gone from green to blue
to violet, but a sparkle, white
in each iris blends to become
yellow, broad brushstrokes
that are the shades of his face

Sampson My Brother

Dad used to yell at him, words
Pulling him back by his long hair
But he was quick out the door
Locks trailing in the wind
When he was a boy he once heard
That brushing hair makes it grow
So he grew his into a fortress
On which he could plant a flag
And he stood strong and proud
Until one day when cancer took his
Head into its lap, and ever so gently
Brushed his hair until it all fell out

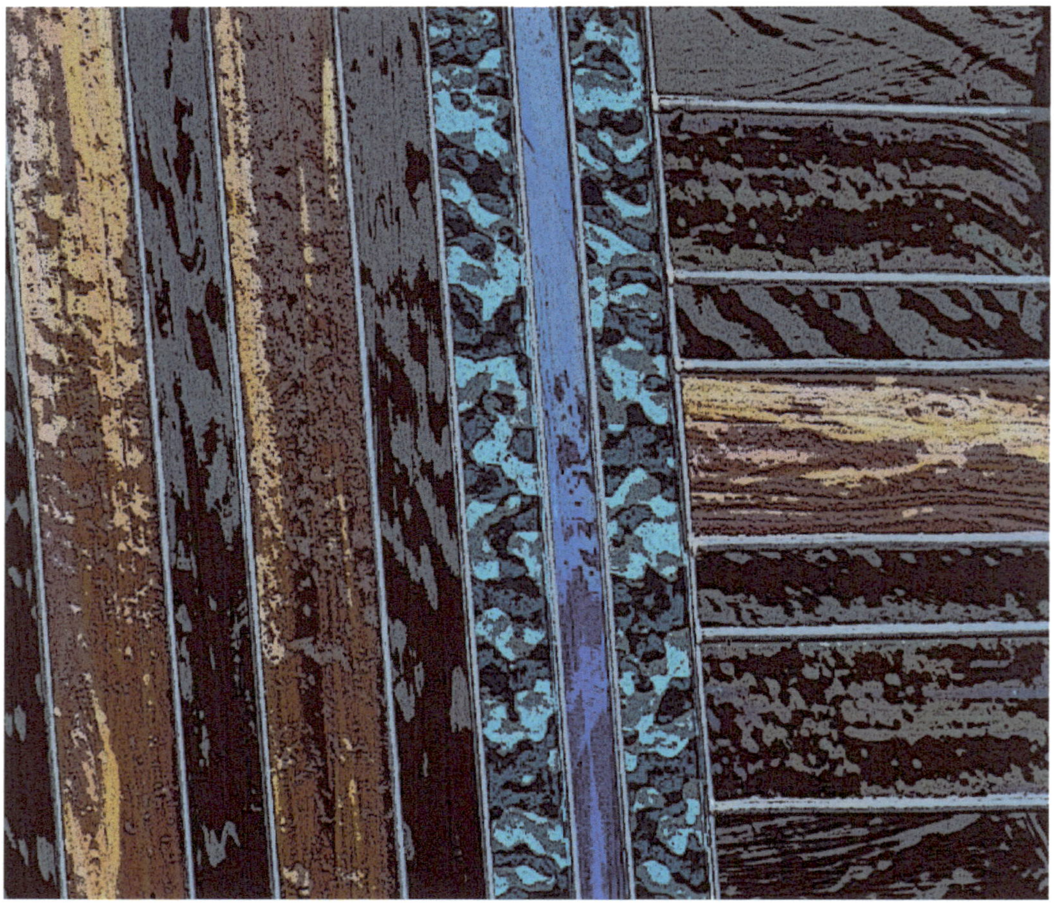

Drive. Stop. Drive.

sometimes one must stop
and watch closely
the tops of trees
as the breeze
passes gentle fingers
through the weakest limbs

while driving once
across an expansion bridge
through the fog
i was greeted by
disembodied smokestacks
bellowing steam
above the clouds

imagine a line
like a steel wire
connecting the rose
to the farthest star
but engage with care
lest you float into space

Cost of Living

Molested, impregnated,
giving birth at fifteen,
a mother thrice over.
switching men, like jobs
for the hopeless, the dreamless
the dark–skinned.

A life bought on minimum wage,
a stone heart and a love
of the grave at thirty.
her twelve grand a year,
the real wage of sin,
the price of a soul.

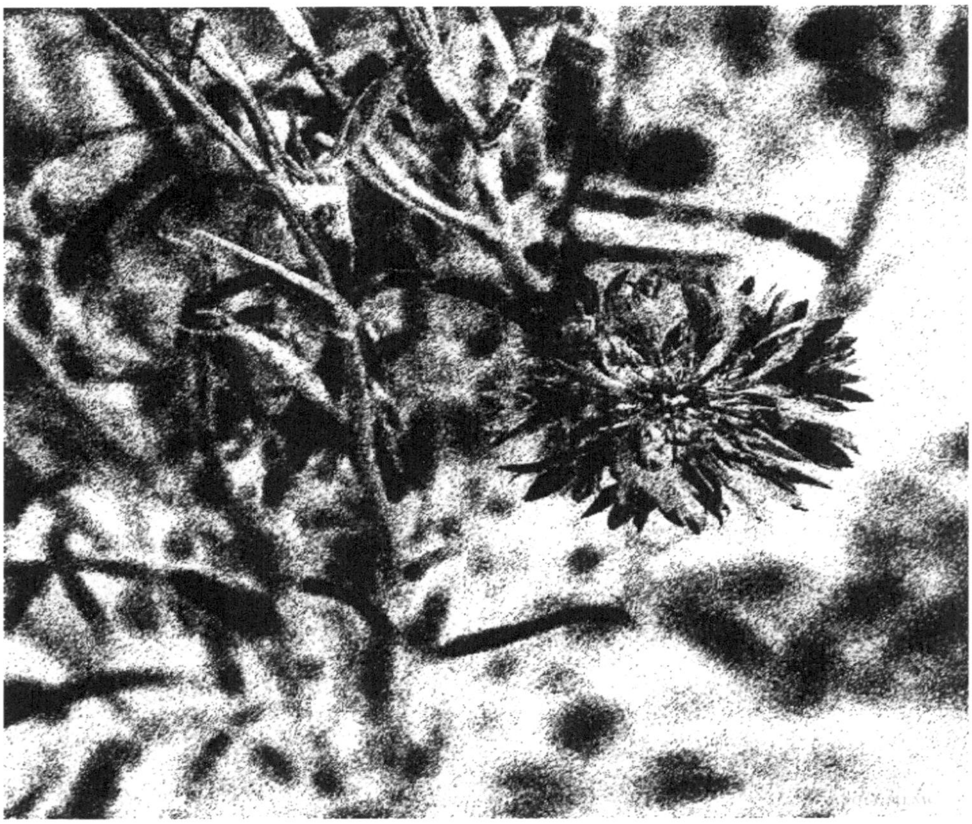

For Willie

he hears the crack
of wood on leather
up it soars
instinct tells him
run to the right
run to the wall
legs like pistons
leather whips out
to capture
the moment

Wallace in Red Weather

Words once haunted
by white and green,
stones on gold rings,
yellow sun dresses,
blue–blood speech
the power
of rhinestones.

Now he sings with
periwinkle
guitars,
thoughts drifts like a sailor
and sleep under stars.

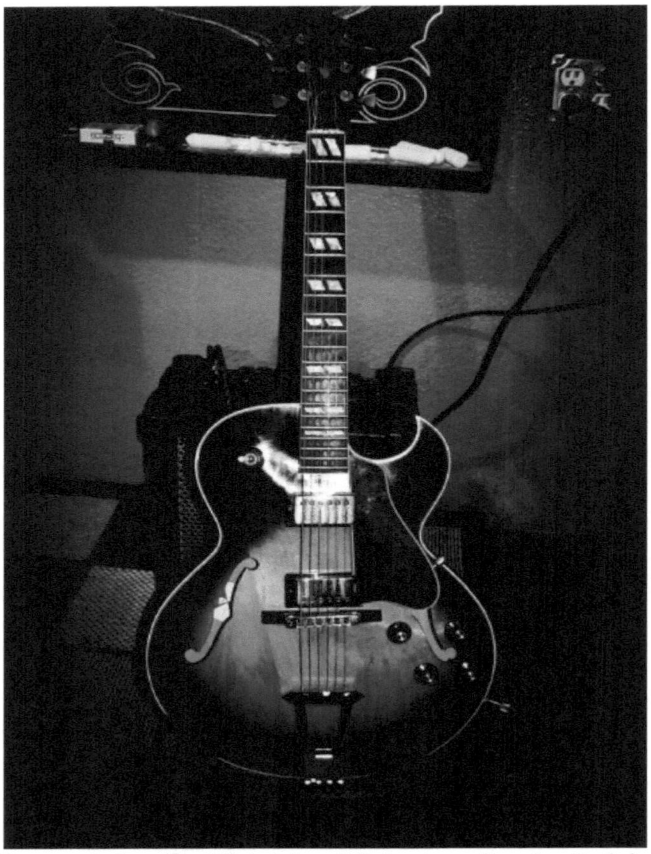

Two Boys in Karbala

When he was twelve years old,
he did his father's bidding,
afraid of the old man's anger.
After all, they were invaders.
They would take his world by force.
They would kill his neighbors.
The other boy, twenty–one,
his uncle handed him total discretion
in life and death decisions, and
afraid of the ambush,
afraid of the young boy's rummaging,
he simply acted, pulled the trigger.

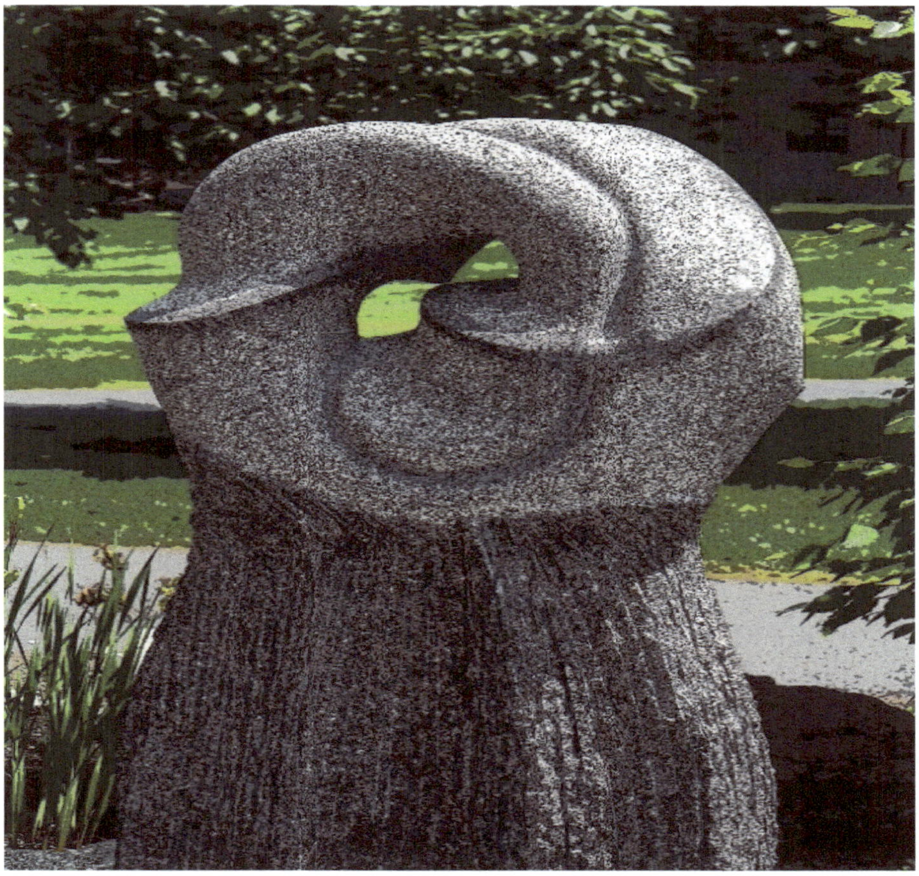

King Street

If you're going to walk
Down king street
Your eyes must be open
You head held high
Beware the sidewalks
They are paved with pitfalls
Fumes of oppression
Will fill the skies

If you're going to own
Your own journey
Be aware of the place
Where you stand
Cluttered paths will clear
As by magic if
You remember some
Slight of hand

Once you've crossed it
The sacred pathway
Once you've reached there
The other side
Roars of lizards
Long gone ages
Fade to silence
As you go by

The path's end
Is your destination, but
Your eyes must be open
You must hold your head high
Journey's end is but a list
Of overwhelming questions
The only answer is this:
The big why

Morning Mirror

Creases
Drawn by dreams of the day before
Etched into this stranger's face
A reflection not quite recognizable
The name seems familiar,
The face escapes…
I have walked into the funhouse
Emotions stretched, disproportionate
Or multiplied infinitely, perhaps a smile
Knowing and mocking
Eyes retreating farther
Into the shadows
Not wanting to see
Into the abyss

Thoughts ride the creases like tracks
Through a private hall of mirrors
For now, they are free
Of the signs of moral decay
Safe from the impending
Collapse of time

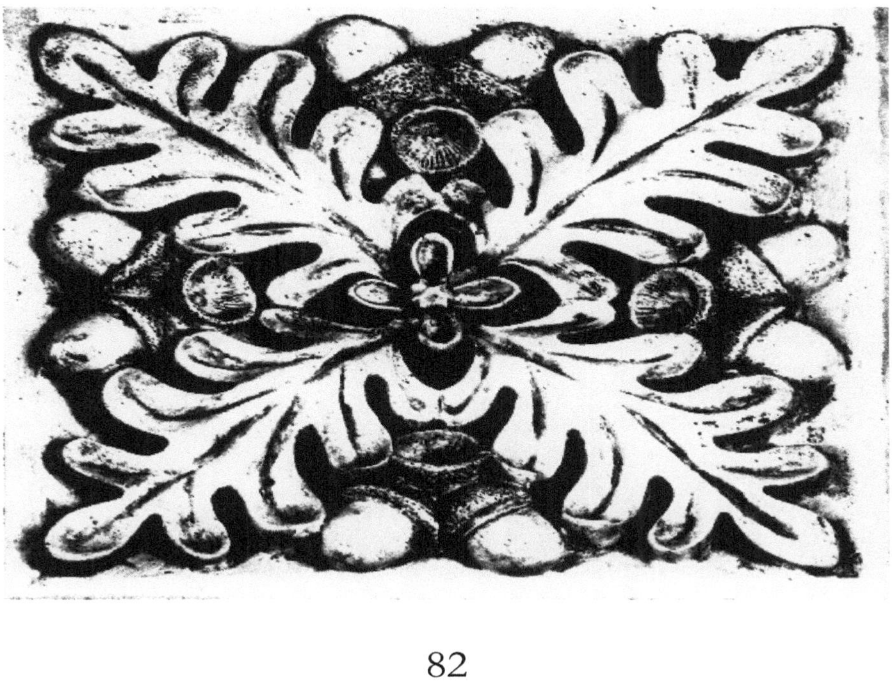

About the Author and Photographer

Now living quite a reclusive life among very close friends and a Fire Oscar named Ringo in the Happy Valley of Western Massachusetts, **M. A. Katz-Savoy** was born and raised on all three American coasts, meanwhile having earned various degrees in music composition, pop culture, and literature, and becoming an avid researcher of beat poetry, philosophy, Beatles songs, ghosts, and vampires (at one point becoming one of only 400 or so vampirologists in the United States, quite by accident).

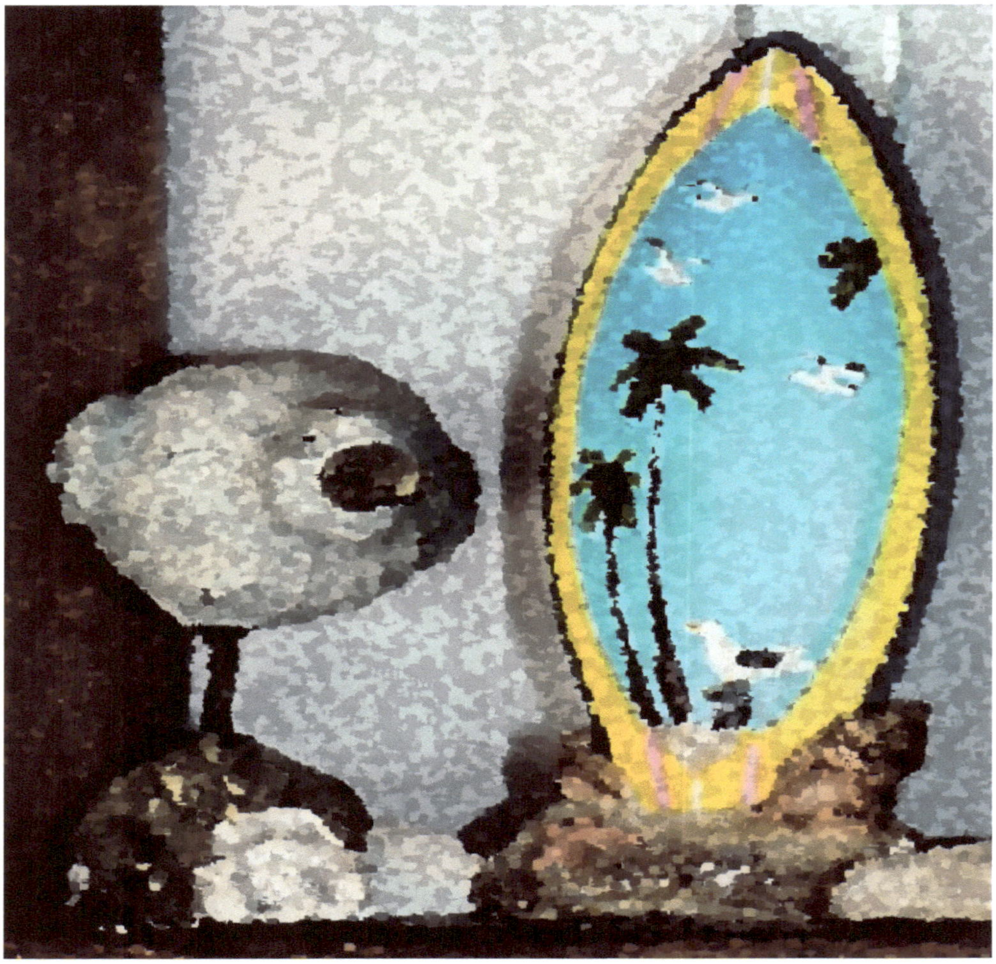

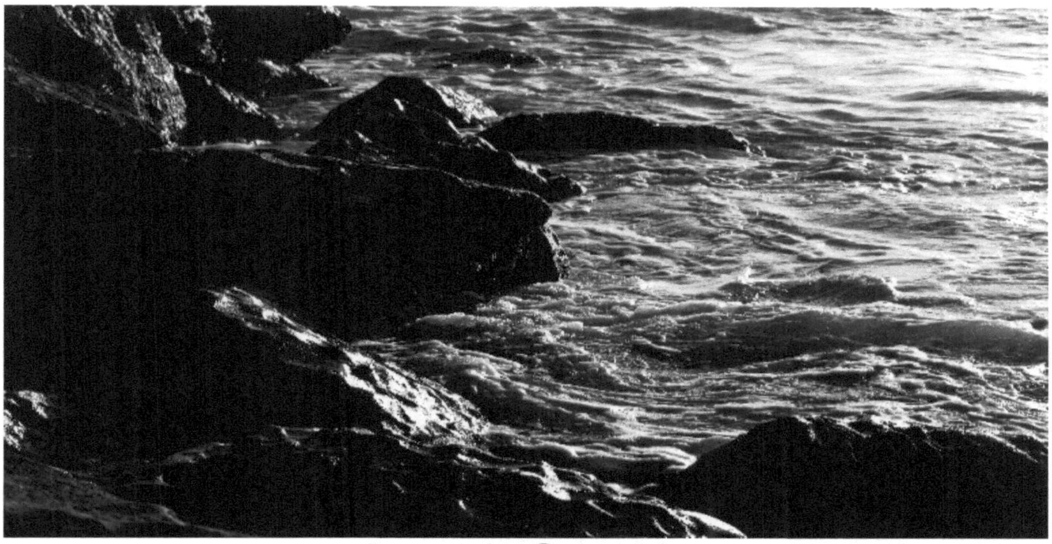

Kristina L. A. Schlah is an American/Canadian who was born in Santa Barbara, California. Currently based in San Buenaventura, a coastal community within reach of all entertainment industry meccas in Southern California, she works with local and international clientele. Her keenly focused eye is an artistic camera lens, and she sees pictures everywhere and in everything. Her media work ranges in style from modern to timeless, and includes formats such as black and white, color, still photography, video, and moving pictures. Her portfolio includes promotional and publicity photography and video work, as well as extensive work on music videos, nationally viewed commercials, presidential re–election campaign media, and public service announcements for domestic violence awareness. Her still photography has received numerous public showings.

If you are interested in purchasing or finding out more about Kristina L. A. Schlah's photography, filmmaking and videomaking, as well as other work, please visit her website, at http://www.klaswork.com.

www.ingramcontent.com/pod-product-compliance
Lightning Source LLC
LaVergne TN
LVHW071057210826
846010LV00055B/107
9781633280045